The Journey

Always Breaking Limitations

By Wai Hung Ma, Corey Sigvaldason, and Kirk Baethke

CAP Publishing
a subsidiary of:
CAP Leadership Solutions Institute Ltd.

#445, 230-1210 Summit Dr.
Kamloops, BC, Canada V2C 6M1

www.CAPLeadership.com

The Journey

Always Breaking Limitations

By Wai Hung Ma, Corey Sigvaldason, and Kirk Baethke

© 2019 Wai Hung Ma, Corey Sigvaldason, Kirk Baethke

All rights reserved. In accordance with international copyright acts, the scanning, uploading, and electronic sharing of any part of this book without permission of the publisher constitute unlawful piracy and theft of the authors' intellectual property. If you would like to use material from the book (other than for review purposes) prior written permission must be obtained by contacting the publisher at info@CAPLeadership.com. Thank you for your support of the authors' rights.

Table of Contents

About this book i

Acknowledgements iii

Support for "The Journey" Book and Testimonials iv

Introduction 1

Wai's Story 5

Acceptance 13

Purpose 21

Goals and Goal Setting 47

Vision 53

Value of a Plan 65

Believe 71

Change 81

Choices 95

Being Responsible.......................... 101

Commitment to Excellence 107

Grit 123

Challenge 133

Growth Mindset 145

Power of our Words and Vocabulary
.... 155

Results 163

Priorities and Wake Up Calls 185

Wai 2.0 and Legacy 195

Final Thoughts 203

Call to Action 217

Authors 219

Booking Keynotes, Other Books, and
Resources 225

About this book

This book is a collection of success concepts to help people overcome obstacles and challenges so they can enjoy living into the "WHAT IF" potential in their lives. It follows the inspirational journey of Wai Hung Ma and his incredible story of breaking limitations and living a life of purpose, meaningfulness, contribution, and optimism while attracting possibilities and tapping the potential we all have within us. Backed by scientific research along with evidence from world-class trainers Corey Sigvaldason and Kirk Baethke, this book combines an uplifting narrative with well-grounded principles that people from all circumstances can utilize to maximize their potential – and success – ultimately leading them to happier and more fulfilling lives.

We all face challenges, obstacles, and failures in life, but the choices we make and mindset we take into them is what ultimately determines our happiness and success. Concepts addressed in the book include:

Acceptance, Purpose, Vision, Goals and Goal Setting, Believing, Change, Choices, Being Responsible, Grit, Challenge, Growth Mindset, and Commitment to Excellence. These concepts are explored through the research and evidence-based approach of Corey's PhD work along with the strong narrative and inspiration from Wai and his journey. This book will not only motivate, but also give you concrete tools to move from just "managing" your life to thriving and unlocking all the potential locked inside you!

Acknowledgements

We would like to thank everyone who has helped us as we created this book; we have been extremely lucky to find the right people.

First, we thank our families for their love and support in all we do. Your dedication to us and your support of everything we do is humbly appreciated. The sacrifices you have made and continue to make help us realize our dreams and, for that, we are forever grateful.

For all our clients past, present, and future, we thank you for affording us the time to pursue our passion and we love to see the impact it has not only in your lives but also those of all the people you positively influence. Together we can all change the world!

With gratitude,

Wai Hung Ma, Corey Sigvaldason, and Kirk Baethke

Support for "The Journey" Book and Testimonials

"We were truly inspired by Wai's story and empowering message. His presentation was dynamic and entertaining - many of the students commented afterwards about how much they really enjoyed it! Everyone could learn something from Wai's perseverance, determination, and positivity. We look forward to hosting another presentation by Wai." - Leanne Mihalicz and Saskia Stinson, Instructors at Thompson Rivers University, Education & Skills Training Program

The Journey
Always Breaking Limitations
By Wai Hung Ma, Corey Sigvaldason, and Kirk Baethke

Introduction

This book follows the narrative and story of Wai Hung Ma and it features some of the principles he's learned on his personal journey to date. It also includes research that supports the concepts and stories Wai introduces while at the same time utilizing Kirk Baethke's leadership experience plus Corey Sigvaldason's business and leadership acumen as well as his PhD research in the area of high performance. We've tried to make the supporting academic research easy to understand, implement, and share with others. Our goal is to not just inspire you with the story and ideas from the book; our dream is to bring out the most in you and your potential – and help you always break limitations!

Wai will share stories from his personal journey and how he continually overcomes challenges in his life. By sharing in his experiences, you will learn the skills to cope with and overcome the challenges in your own life. One thing we know for certain: everyone faces challenges. The key is knowing how to deal with them. Born with cerebral palsy and facing many of his own person trials, Wai's desire to inspire people to overcome their difficulties led him to become an author, motivational speaker, song writer, and advocate for people with special needs.

Wai has chosen a career in speaking despite there being a time when many doubted he would even be able to carry on a basic conversation. Wai is surrounded by a great support structure of family and friends who are inspired by his attitude and determination to make a difference in others lives by sharing his experience.

Wai currently has two books ("Breaking Limitations" and "Motivation"), a song of his became a country music video in 1997, and he is now delivering his keynote presentations titled "Breaking Limitations", "How To Become A Better Bully," and now, "The Journey: Always Breaking Limitations."

Wai is committed to equality and peace for all people. He is passionate about social justice, global education, and is a model teacher in his own right. His message will permeate all audiences and ages.

With the help of technology and his coach and best friend Corey Sigvaldason, Kirk Baethke and CAP Leadership, as well as many others, Wai is living his dream.

Wai's Story

We know 100% of the people reading this book have experienced crisis at some point in their life. Only one person has the power to control your emotions and your feelings as you work through a crisis – that person is you!

Let's begin our journey by introducing you to Wai – as seen through his own eyes:

> *"I was born in Hong Kong and I was born with the neurological disorder cerebral palsy - which means that some parts of my body don't function properly. For starters, I can't walk; I use a wheelchair to get around most of the time. I can't use one of my hands. I also have a speech impediment that not only makes me talk funny, it*

makes it difficult for many people to understand me.

"When I was 11, my whole family moved from Hong Kong to Canada so I might have a better life. You see, people in Hong Kong view disabilities differently compared to Canadians. People back in Hong Kong looked down on me and others that have challenges. The stereotype they had of me was that I must be stupid.

"It was hard to move to Canada because I quickly had to learn how to speak a new language and adapt to English culture. I felt I had to prove to people that I wasn't, and still am not, stupid and I can learn just like anyone else. All I needed was a bit of help.

"I received that help from some great teachers. I went on to graduate high school and then moved on to university. Ever since I was young, I always pushed myself to do my best and to break limitations. I have always strived to reach over and beyond things that stand in my way and find a path to my dreams. Some examples of this are: learning English as a second language, adapting to a new culture, learning to horseback ride so I could take part in a week-long cattle drive, learning to ski, and learning to swim long distances for exercise. Most importantly, despite my speech impediment, I've become a professional speaker and trainer. I'll keep reaching for greater and greater heights; to break

> *limitations and use my story to inspire others to do the same."*

Clearly, Wai and his story form a great backdrop against which we can talk about breaking limitations and working through challenges. Wai's desire to inspire people to overcome their difficulties led him to become what he is today – author, motivational speaker, song writer, and advocate for youth and adults with special needs.

Wai is a man who continually lives his life by breaking limitations. However, Wai doesn't let any of those limitations prevent him from moving into his "what if" potential.

From his personal journey, Wai says:

> *"Floating here, feeling the cool water all over my body...going back and forth along the length of the pool...nobody can understand how my body and*

mind experiences this. Each person experiences things differently. No two people can feel the same.

"Let me tell you about my experience. I hadn't been in a pool for twenty years. On May 12, 2015, I managed to swim two lengths, which is equal to a single 100-meter lap. I need to be able to do 39 more laps to reach my fundraiser goal, so I tried to train twice a week at the YMCA pool. Three lifeguards - Hope Hacquoil,

Meghan Fair and Tanya Hamelock - volunteered to be on my team.

"Each time people enter my life they have taught me things, then they have had to go. I'm not weaker because they leave, I'm stronger. It's time for the next person to enter my life. This is how the real world works. We need to accept change as a part of life. I know change is hard, but it is a good thing. It gives us a chance to learn new things that we otherwise would never would."

Living is about learning. It makes us grow.

We want to share some of the lessons Wai has learned that he feels can be of value to you. As we cover these lessons, you're encouraged to think of where this may apply in your life.

Think about how you might use these lessons to break through your own limitations and live into your "what if" potential.

Acceptance

"Accept what you are, who you are, and how you do things in your own way.

"We have no choice how we enter this world. We do what we have to, to make a better life for ourselves. Do I wish I can walk? My answer would be no. All I know is how to be in a wheelchair and how to deal with a speech impediment. There is no way I can change these facts. I have to find my own way to do everything, all my life.

"Acceptance does not mean 'giving up'. Acceptance means finding a different path to get to where you want to be. People can't keep banging their heads

against the wall. It will never work; the wall will beat you every time. You need to find a new way to get over the wall. We have to think logically and creatively. I have been doing this all my life, finding creative ways to overcome my obstacles. I reach for where I want to be.

"People cannot change their DNA no matter how hard they try. They should work with what they are born with. We have to accept. We cannot change how we are born into the world. There is no way to change the facts. You have to accept what you are before you can go forward. One cannot change what one is born with. You can change your appearance, but it is impossible to change what you are born into.

"On the other hand, a person can change their spirit. What kind of a person do you want to be? Our life is full of questions, it is our job to find the answers to them. Nobody can find the answers for us, but us. Nobody truly knows what we want, but us."

(Wai Hung Ma, 2018)

There's nobody out there that's completely ready for something truly awful to happen to them. Suddenly, an able-bodied person becomes disabled; maybe they lose their legs and can't walk or get around like they used to. But, through persistence and acceptance, anyone can overcome victim thinking and move on. Take Wai for example. He has a speech impediment, but he's become a professional speaker! He accepted his difficulty with speaking as an unalterable fact about himself and was persistent in leveraging the people and knowledge around him to achieve his goal. Wai is who he is, he's accepted that, and has achieved a life goal as a result.

When it comes to accepting others, German philosopher Johann Wolfgang von Goethe put it so beautifully: *"If you treat an individual as he is, he will remain so. But if you treat him as if he were what he ought to be and could be, he will become what he ought to be and could be."*

In other words, treat people as though they are what they ought to be and help them be capable of what they are becoming.

See the light in people. People can teach you so much once you accept who they are. The power of one will always lead to the power of many. We see this all the time in the corporate training and consulting we do. Wai sees it in the team around him as well as when he's speaking and inspiring people everywhere.

Now, of course, life isn't always fair. But with the power of acceptance, we can choose to enter a state of adaptability. Psychologist Anders Ericsson, in his 2016 best selling book Peak, refers to adaptability as "the gift." He does so to demonstrate it is not an innate talent we are born with per se that is a gift but rather the ability for all of us to adapt through purposeful practice. We know this also means you have a choice - get bitter or get better.

As Drago Adams from the Oct 16, 2016, Monday Morning Motivator Newsletter said:

"It's like the typical story of being an entrepreneur: the first part happens fast. You throw yourself into establishing a business, and you're out on the water; the shore is pushing off behind you and the trees are getting smaller. The distant shore doesn't seem so far, and you can feel the resolution coming, the feeling of getting out of your boat and walking the distant beach. You think it's going to happen fast, you'll paddle for a bit and arrive on the other side by lunch. But the truth is, it isn't going to be over soon.

"The work is harder than you imagined. But the point is not just about getting to the other side or

achieving your visions and seeing results. It's much more about your character getting molded in the hard work of the middle.

"At some point the shore behind you stops getting smaller, and you paddle and wonder why the same strokes that used to move you now only rock the boat. You made the network and got influence through business, but you just don't know if you have enough to make it through.

"You'd rather work for someone else, and live a common life, because the far shore doesn't get closer no matter how hard you paddle. The shore you left is just as distant, and there is no going back; there is only the decision to paddle in place or stop, slide out of the hatch, and sink into the sea.

"When something hard happens to you, you have two choices in how to

deal with it. You can either get bitter or better."

The lesson here is summed up nicely in a bible verse from Galatians 6:9: "don't get weary of doing good, for in due season you will reap, if you do not give up." Accept the facts, utilize your adaptability, and find your path to success.

Purpose

For decades, psychologists, authors, and researchers have studied how long-term, meaningful goals develop over time. The kinds of goals that foster a strong sense of purpose are ones that can potentially change the lives of other people, goals like launching an organization, researching a disease, or teaching kids to read. Many of those we admire or who inspire us do so because of their deep sense of purpose and the mission they set out on to answer their calling in life.

Indeed, a sense of purpose appears to have evolved in humans so we can accomplish big things together – which may be why it's associated with better physical and mental health. Purpose is adaptive, in an evolutionary sense. It helps both individuals - and the species - survive.

This examination of sense of purpose leads us to also look at the concept of motivation – the thing that drives a person to do something. What motivates you to reach your goals? Alternatively, how do you arrive at setting goals you are truly motivated to achieve? What's the criteria for deciding which goals to reach for? How do you define your goals?

Everything we do has a purpose – and that gives us sufficient reason (motivation) for reaching our goals. If we don't have a good enough reason, why should we even bother to do our best or try to reach our goals; what's the point in trying, right? We need something to drive us forward as we reach for whatever it is we want for ourselves or others. Purpose lives within almost every part of our existence.

What am I designed to do? What do I desire to do? What do I have a unique ability to do? Most people ask themselves some version of these questions at some point. However, far too many move on without a real answer. Let's look at "The 3 D's of Purpose":

What is your DESIGN?

What is your DESIRE?

What is your DISTINCTION?

If you're struggling to discover your purpose, asking - and honestly answering - these questions will help give you the awareness you need to help you find the purpose in your life.

A few years ago, Wai decided to raise funds for the YMCA Women's Shelter in his "Swim All The Wai" fundraiser by swimming two kilometers. We all agreed that this was a great cause for the common good in our community; this was Wai's outward purpose. But his inner purpose was that he wanted people to get to know him and how driven he is.

By doing so, people might be inspired to buy his books and come to his workshops. Wai felt it was a way to help the community but at the same time market himself. Wai realized he needed a purpose and an inner drive. Motivation is about reward. In fact, everything is about reward and payoff. Without rewards and payoffs, nothing can move forward.

Many seem to believe that purpose arises from "special gifts" which set you apart from other people, but that's only part of the story. Purpose also grows from our connection to others, which is why a crisis of purpose is often a symptom of isolation.

Research from the University of Southern California Berkley outlines six ways to overcome isolation and discover your purpose in life[1]:

1. Read

Reading connects us to people we'll never know, across time and space—an experience that research says is linked to a sense of meaning and purpose. (Note: "Meaning" and "purpose" are linked but separate social-scientific constructs. Purpose is a part of meaning; meaning is a much broader concept that usually

---

[1]https://greatergood.berkeley.edu/article/item/how_to_find_your_purpose_in_life (May 6, 2019)

also includes value, efficacy, and self-worth.)

In a 2010 paper, for example, Leslie Francis studied a group of nearly 26,000 teenagers throughout England and Wales—and found that those who read the Bible more tended to have a stronger sense of purpose. Secular reading seems to make a difference, as well. In a survey of empirical studies, Raymond A. Mar and colleagues found a link between reading poetry and fiction and a sense of purpose among adolescents.

"Reading fiction might allow adolescents to reason about the whole lives of characters, giving them specific insight into an entire lifespan without having to have fully lived most of their own lives," they suggest. By seeing purpose in the lives of other people, teens are more likely to see it in their own lives. In this sense, purpose is an act of the imagination.

Many people interviewed for this article mentioned pivotal books or ideas they found in books.

The writing of historian W.E.B. Du Bois pushed social-justice activist Art McGee to embrace a specific vision of African-American identity and liberation. Journalist Michael Stoll found inspiration in the "social responsibility theory of journalism," which he read about at Stanford University. "Basically, reporters and editors have not just the ability but also the duty to improve their community by being independent arbiters of problems that need solving," he says. "It's been my professional North Star ever since." Spurred by this idea, Michael went on to launch an award-winning non-profit news agency called The San Francisco Public Press.

So, if you're feeling a crisis of purpose in your life, go to the bookstore or library or university. Find books that matter to you—and they might help you to see what matters in your own life.

2. Turn hurts into healing for others

Of course, finding purpose is not just an intellectual pursuit; it's something we need to feel. That's why it can grow out of suffering, both our own and others'.

Kezia Willingham was raised in poverty in Corvallis, Oregon, her family riven by domestic violence. "No one at school intervened or helped or supported my mother, myself, or my brother when I was growing up poor, ashamed, and sure that my existence was a mistake," she says. "I was running the streets, skipping school, having sex with strangers, and abusing every drug I could get my hands on."

When she was 16, Kezia enrolled at an alternative high school that "led me to believe I had options and a path out of poverty." She made her way to college and was especially "drawn to the kids with 'issues'"—kids like the one she had once been. She says:

I want the kids out there who grew up like me, to know they have futures ahead of them. I want them to know they are smart, even if they may not meet state academic standards. I want them to know that they are just as good and valuable as any other human who happens to be born into more privileged circumstances. Because they are. And there are so damn many messages telling them otherwise.

Sometimes, another person's pain can lead us to purpose. When Christopher Pepper was a senior in high school, a "trembling, tearful friend" told him that she had been raped by a classmate. "I comforted as well as I could, and left that conversation vowing that I would do something to keep this from happening to others," says Christopher. He kept that promise by becoming a Peer Rape Educator in college—and then a sex educator in San Francisco public schools.

Why do people like Kezia and Christopher seem to find purpose in suffering—while others are crushed by it? Part of the answer, as we'll see next, might have to do with the emotions and behaviors we cultivate in ourselves.

3. Cultivate awe, gratitude, and altruism

Certain emotions and behaviors that promote health and well-being can also foster a sense of purpose—specifically, awe, gratitude, and altruism.

Several studies conducted by the Greater Good Science Center's Dacher Keltner have shown that the experience of awe makes us feel connected to something larger than ourselves—and so can provide the emotional foundation for a sense of purpose.

Of course, awe all by itself won't give you a purpose in life. It's not enough to just feel like you're a small part of something big; you also need to feel driven to make a positive impact on the world. That's where gratitude and generosity come into play.

"It may seem counterintuitive to foster purpose by cultivating a grateful mindset, but it works," writes psychologist Kendall Bronk, a leading expert on purpose. As research by William Damon, Robert Emmons, and others has found, children and adults who are able to count their blessings are much

more likely to try to "contribute to the world beyond themselves." This is probably because, if we can see how others make our world a better place, we'll be more motivated to give something back.

Here we arrive at altruism. There's little question, at this point, that helping others is associated with a meaningful, purposeful life. In one study, for example, Daryl Van Tongeren and colleagues found that people who engage in more altruistic behaviors, like volunteering or donating money, tend to have a greater sense of purpose in their lives.

Interestingly, gratitude and altruism seem to work together to generate meaning and purpose. In a second experiment, the researchers randomly assigned some participants to write letters of gratitude—and those people later reported a stronger sense of purpose. More recent work by

Christina Karns and colleagues found that altruism and gratitude are neurologically linked, activating the same reward circuits in the brain

4. Listen to what other people appreciate about you

Giving thanks can help you find your purpose. But you can also find purpose in what people thank you for.

Like Kezia Willingham, Shawn Taylor had a tough childhood—and he was also drawn to working with kids who had severe behavioral problems. Unlike her, however, he often felt like the work was a dead-end. "I thought I sucked at my chosen profession," he says. Then, one day, a girl he'd worked with five years before contacted him.

"She detailed how I helped to change her life," says Shawn—and she asked him to walk her down the aisle when she got married. Shawn hadn't even

thought about her, in all that time. "Something clicked and I knew this was my path. No specifics, but youth work was my purpose."

The artists, writers, and musicians I interviewed often described how appreciation from others fueled their work. Dani Burlison never lacked a sense of purpose, and she toiled for years as a writer and social-justice activist in Santa Rosa, California. But when wildfires swept through her community, Dani discovered that her strengths were needed in a new way: "I've found that my networking and emergency response skills have been really helpful to my community, my students, and to firefighters!"

Although there is no research that directly explores how being thanked might fuel a sense of purpose, we do know that gratitude strengthens relationships—and those are often the source of our purpose, as many of these stories suggest.

5. Find and build community

As we see in Dani's case, we can often find our sense of purpose in the people around us.

Many people told me about finding purpose in family. In tandem with his reading, Art McGee found purpose—working for social and racial justice—in "love and respect for my hardworking father," he says. "Working people like him deserved so much better."

Environmental and social-justice organizer Jodi Sugerman-Brozan feels driven "to leave the world in a better place than I found it." Becoming a mom "strengthened that purpose (it's going to be their world, and their kids' world)," she says. It "definitely influences how I parent (wanting to raise anti-racist, feminist, radical kids who will want to continue the fight and be leaders)."

Of course, our kids may not embrace our purpose. Amber Cantorna was raised by purpose-driven parents who were right-wing Christians. "My mom had us involved in stuff all the time, all within that conservative Christian bubble," she says. This family and community fueled a strong sense of purpose in Amber: "To be a good Christian and role model. To be a blessing to other people."

The trouble is that this underlying purpose involved making other people more like them. When she came out as a lesbian at age 27, Amber's family and community swiftly and suddenly cast her out. This triggered a deep crisis of purpose—one that she resolved by finding a new faith community "that helped shape me and gave me a sense of belonging," she says.

Often, the nobility of our purpose reflects the company we keep. The purpose that came from Amber's parents was based on exclusion, as she discovered. There was no place—and no purpose—for her in that community once she embraced an identity they couldn't accept. A new sense of purpose came with the new community and identity she helped to build, of gay and lesbian Christians.

If you're having trouble remembering your purpose, take a look at the people around you. What do you have in common with them? What are they trying to be? What impact do you see them having on the world? Is that impact a positive one? Can you join with them in making that impact? What do they need? Can you give it them?

If the answers to those questions don't inspire you, then you might need to find a new community—and with that, a new purpose may come.

6. *Tell your story*

Reading can help you find your purpose—but so can writing,

Purpose often arises from curiosity about your own life. What obstacles have you encountered? What strengths helped you to overcome them? How did other people help you? How did your strengths help make life better for others?

"We all have the ability to make a narrative out of our own lives," says Emily Esfahani Smith, author of the 2017 book The Power of Meaning. *"It gives us clarity on our own lives, how to understand ourselves, and gives us a framework that goes beyond the day-to-day and basically helps us make sense of our experiences."*

That's why Amber Cantorna wrote her memoir, Refocusing My Family: Coming Out, Being Cast Out, and Discovering the True Love of God. *At first depressed after losing everyone she loved, Amber soon discovered new strengths in herself—and she is using her book to help build a non-profit organization called Beyond to support gay, lesbian, bisexual, and transgender Christians in their coming-out process.*

One 2008 study found that those who see meaning and purpose in their lives are able to tell a story of change and growth, where they managed to overcome the obstacles they encountered. In other words, creating a narrative like Amber's can help us to see our own strengths and how applying those strengths can make a difference in the world, which increases our sense of self-efficacy.

This is a valuable reflective process to all people, but Amber took it one step further, by publishing her autobiography and turning it into a tool for social change. Today, Amber's purpose is to help people like her feel less alone.

"My sense of purpose has grown a lot with my desire to share my story—and the realization that so many other people have shared my journey."

Once you find your path, you'll almost certainly find others traveling along with you hoping to reach the same destination – a community. This is how world-changing movements happen! Great leaders like Mother Teresa, Ghandi, Terry Fox, Rev. Martin Luther King Jr., or even those teachers and parents that made a personal difference to just a single person.

An article we ran across in our reading some time ago (from athletesinaction.org) wrote of a company that didn't believe in sales and revenue goals. Of course, they forecasted sales for budgetary, planning, and growth purposes and measured numbers and outcomes, but they did so with the belief that numbers were just a by-product of how well they were living and sharing their purpose. So, instead of focusing on goals with numbers, the company, Organic Valley, passionately focused on their purpose-driven goals: providing opportunities for farmers to make a living, supporting sustainability of the land, and supplying families with healthy dairy products free of hormones and antibiotics. The result: Organic Valley's sales and revenue kept growing and growing.

In another example, the author of the Organic Valley article, while speaking to an NFL team a few years ago, had each player write their goals on a piece of paper. After a few minutes, inspired by Joshua Medcalf's book Burn Your Goals, he had them rip up the paper they had just written on.

You could imagine the complaints and feel their anger and frustration while they ripped up the paper they had just spent a considerable amount of time and energy writing on. They were then asked, "How many of you wrote down win a Super Bowl, win x number of games, achieve x number of yards, have x number of interceptions, etc.?" Everyone's hands went up.

He told them that every person in every NFL meeting room has the same goals. It's not the goals that will make you successful, otherwise everyone and every team would be successful after writing down their goals. Instead, it's your commitment to the process, your growth, and your purpose that drives you to reach these goals which will determine what you accomplish.

He then had them write down their commitments and purpose for playing and had them share with the rest of the team. It was powerful.

The truth is numbers and goals don't drive people. People with a purpose drive the numbers and achieve goals. Metrics may motivate you in the short-term, but they will not sustain you over time. Without a good reason to keep moving forward during a challenge you either quit or go through the motions. Research in 2013 by psychologists Barrick,

Mount, and Li[2], clearly shows that true motivation is driven by experienced meaningfulness and purpose driven goals rather than extrinsic rewards, numbers, and achievement or performance goals.

This doesn't mean you shouldn't measure numbers or have goals; it's okay to have a goal you want to achieve. But once you identify a goal or outcome, you will be more powerful and energized if you focus on your purpose. The stronger your purpose, the stronger your resolve and will to succeed - and THAT leads to greater performance! One thing that's clear is purpose-driven goals sell more milk, win more football games, enhance performance, and lead to

---

[2] Barrick, M. R., Mount, M. K., & LI, N. (2013). The theory of purposeful work behavior: The role of personality, higher-order goals, and job characteristics. Academy of Management Review, 38(1), 132-153.

outcomes that far surpass your number or achievement goals.

Goals and Goal Setting

If you're reading this book, you might already know that Corey is known for goal-setting, increasing performance, and getting results while improving team cohesion and personal well-being. One of his many blog posts provides perspective on goal-setting from the world's top executive coach, Marshall Goldsmith[3]:

The typical advertisement or "infomercial" – designed to help people "get in shape" – provides a great example of what not to do in goal-setting. The message is almost always the same, "For an 'incredibly small' amount of money – you can buy a 'revolutionary' product – that is 'unbelievably easy' and 'fun to use'.

---

[3]http://www.marshallgoldsmithfeedforward.com/marshallgoldsmithblog/?p=1082&utm_source=03+CBC+Full&utm_campaign=03+CBC+-+Full&utm_medium=email

This product will produce 'amazing results' 'in almost no time' and you will 'have the body that you always wanted'." Most infomercials imply that you will not have to continue exercising and dieting for years – that you will continue to look young – and that you will have frequent, wonderful sex for the rest of your life.

In reality, there is no "easy answer" – real change requires real effort. The "quick fix" is seldom a "meaningful fix". Distractions and competing responses are going to happen and the most successful people, and those who really want to be great, understand this.

Below are three of the most important reasons that people give up on goals followed by a brief description of how successful people "do it differently" and are ultimately well-positioned to achieve their goals.

Ownership One of the biggest mistakes in all of leadership development is the roll-out of programs and initiatives with the promise that "this will make you better". A classic example is the performance appraisal process. Many companies change their performance appraisal forms on a regular basis. How much good does this usually do? None! These appraisal form changes just confuse people and are seen as annual exercises in futility. What companies don't want to face is the real problem – it is seldom the form – the real problem is the managers who lack either the courage or the discipline to make the appraisal process work. The problem with the "this will make you better" approach is that the emphasis is on the "this" and not the "you".

Rather than rely on the latest "program," successful people have a high need for and reliance upon self-determination. They commit to the challenge, task, or process that needs their efforts and make a plan to meet their goals. Because of this commitment, they are far more likely to achieve success.

Time Most of us have a natural tendency to underestimate the time needed to reach targets. Everything seems to take longer than we think that it should! When the time elapsed in working toward our goal starts exceeding expectations, we are tempted to just give up on the goal, and often do.

Successful goal-setters are more time-sensitive than the general population. They are more realistic about the time it will take them to implement and complete various changes and/or tasks. In addition, they review their goals frequently and adjust their plans for progress as necessary. Thus, they are more likely to meet their own goal expectations.

Difficulty The gripe with difficulty is, "The challenge, process, or task is a lot harder than I thought it would be. It sounded so simple when I was starting out!"

In setting goals it is important that we realize that real change will take real work. Expecting that "this will be easy" and "this will be no problem for me" can backfire in the long-term when we realize that change is not easy and that we will invariably face some problems in our journey toward change.

Successful people understand that there will be a price for success – they will have to work hard to achieve their goals. This realistic outlook prevents the disappointment that can occur when challenges do arise later in the change process – and as a result they are less likely to give up.

All of these messages may sound "tough", but they are real. Successful people are not afraid of challenging goals. In fact – clear, specific goals that produce a lot of challenge – tend to produce the best results!

Vision

"The greatest achievement was at first and for a time a dream. The oak sleeps in the acorn; the bird waits in the egg; and in the highest vision of the soul a waking angel stirs. Dreams are the seedlings of reality."

(James Allen, from As a Man Thinketh)

Every great journey begins with a dream. The power of the dream is when you transform it into an inspiring vision which leads you and others to action. The greatest visionaries in history inspired movements because of their vision. Greats like Mother Teresa, Gandhi, Martin Luther King Jr., Terry Fox, and Jesus all had a strong and inspiring vision that compelled them and others to action and in so doing changed the world. As leaders, you need to connect with a strong vision that not only inspires yourself but attracts others to your vision which compels action and starts a movement that sees "game-changing results."

A while back, Corey read an article by John Maxwell titled, "What's Love Got To Do With It?"[4] In the article Maxwell asks great questions like: "Where does vision come from?" "How does a leader develop a clear vision for the future?" Maxwell continues:

---

[4] https://www.johnmaxwell.com/blog/vision-whats-love-got-to-do-with-it/

"At the earliest stages, the word 'vision' may be somewhat misleading, portraying vision as a picture that we can see. The birthplace of vision isn't the mind's eye, but the heart. In the beginning, visionaries are guided by passion not sight. They must feel their way in the dark at first, and only through time do they gain a mental image of what the future could look like.

"Vision is what you want to do in life, not only what you think should be done. I can think of a thousand noble causes, but only a select few resonate with my heart. Vision begins as a compelling want or desire. The genesis of vision isn't purely an intellectual exercise; it involves monitoring your passions.

"Passion generates vision, but I certainly do not recommend blindly following your heart. When developing a vision it's necessary to

realistically assess your strengths, skills, and available opportunities. For example, I may aspire to sing on Broadway, but if the sounds of my voice makes an audience cover their ears in pain, then it's time to focus on another area of passion. Desire alone surely is not sufficient to develop a vision. Yet, every vision starts with an emotional spark."

- Passion Births Vision (John Maxwell)

Wishing for something is not enough to have us reach our potential. Nor is ability alone going to get you there; we're sure you've met or heard of people who had great ability, but never truly capitalized on it or, worse yet, squandered it or took it for granted, got complacent, and fell into mediocrity.

Opportunities will present themselves, but simply seizing the opportunity will never get anyone to the top. Knowledge is a great asset, but often comes up short helping you, as the US army says, "[be] all that you can be." Even great teams and support structures, although important, are insufficient on their own. None of the above can operate in a bubble. Vision that translates into a relentless and driving passion is the real difference-maker.

We haven't seen an individual reach their potential and change the world without first having a strong vision that fuels their passion. Horst Schultze, former COO of the Ritz Carlton says:

"You are nothing unless it comes from your heart. Passion, caring, really looking to create excellence. If you perform functions only and go to work only to do processes, then you are effectively retired. And it scares me - most people I see, by age 28, are

retired... If you go to work only to fulfill the processes and functions then you are a machine. You have to bring passion, commitment and caring - then you are a human being."

As children we were constantly dreaming and daydreaming. Our imaginations were limitless, and creativity was unstoppable. We literally behaved and believed at times we were superheroes. The reality is – we still are superheroes. We still have that ability to save people and make the world a better place through our contribution. So, what are your superpowers? What is that inspiring vision that gives you and those you impact supernatural powers? When you connect to that, you begin to change the world. Without it, we stop dreaming and settle for survival. We relinquish heartfelt vision in exchange for security and comfort. Please don't do that. The world needs that superhero inside you.

Let's go back to John Maxwell for a moment. Also included in that article was an interesting and enlightening research study that drives home the results of living a life driven by vision and inner purpose. In the study, a team of researchers followed a group of 1,500 MBA's over a period of 20 years. To start, the participants were divided into two groups.

Group A, 83 percent of the sample, was composed of people who were embarking on a career path that they had chosen solely for the prospect of making money now in order to do what they wanted later in life. Group B, the other 17 percent of the sample, consisted of people who had chosen their career path so they could do what they wanted to do now and worry about the money later.

The data showed some startling revelations:

• At the end of the 20-year period, 101 of the 1,500 had become millionaires.

• Of the millionaires, all but one - 100 out of 101 - were from Group B, the group that had chosen to pursue what they loved.

In summarizing the research for his book Getting Rich Your Own Way, Srully Blotnick observed the following:

"A missing ingredient had to be present if someone was going to become rich: they had to find their work absorbing. Involving. Enthralling."

The success stories choose passion over predictable earnings. They had a vision for life beyond material riches, and ironically, they ended up generating the most wealth.

To birth a vision, begin by paying attention to your areas of passion. What makes you feel alive? What matters the most to you in life? What activities can absorb your attention for hours? Don't worry about being able to see the whole picture immediately. As you look for ways to make contributions doing what you love, eventually a picture will emerge in your mind of how you can shape the future.

Corey wrote a blog post some years ago titled "Guidepost or Hitching Post" and in it we find additional wisdom for visionaries and those who wish to change the world. The premise: we all need to decide if are we a guidepost or are we a hitching post. Let's explain.

When people talk about change, they either embrace it, fight it, or roll with it. As leaders and businesspeople, we believe we have a greater responsibility in managing change (or more appropriately responding to change). Anyone who says they are not subject to change is hallucinating.

Great leaders have vision that capitalizes on change and often creates the future. Corey talked of change this way with a friend a while back:

"A wise man once asked, 'Is your business attached to a hitching post or a guidepost?' If your business is attached to a hitching post, you remain fixed, bound to your past, unable to move forward. If your business is attached to a guidepost, your business is free to learn from the past and form values that will keep you on track as you progress. So, I ask – is your business attached to a hitching post or a guidepost?"

As a leader and business make sure you are attached to a guidepost.

Wai's vision is to continue to challenge himself in physical pursuits as well as contributions goals he has. He is now expanding outward from his regional market and looking to take his message and inspiration globally. Wai is living out his vision and being a guidepost!

Value of a Plan

Last chapter we concluded with Wai's vision to go global now. He has a plan and is keenly aware of the importance and value of a plan.

Corey once spoke at a Salmon Arm, British Columbia, Downtown Improvement Association annual general meeting on "How To Position Your Business In Changing Times." Through his research he interviewed a local businesswoman and got her insights on how she has successfully positioned herself. Cookie, the owner of Culinary Inspirations, started her business just before Halloween 2008 – right the start of a major economic downturn. Further, she was starting a business in a community that relies heavily on a robust summer tourism season. Despite those challenges, her business has been profitable every month and has grown her business twenty percent per year. Cookie, plus all her great staff, have done so well primarily due to two reasons (although she's quick to admit that much of her success is part instinct and part living by the golden rule!)

First, she had created a corporate culture and atmosphere that is customer-focused, kind, and respectful. People are greeted as they come into her store and acknowledged as they leave -always done with a smile and enthusiasm. Customers love going in because it feels like they're coming home. She also responds to her customers and requests with personalized service that make all her customers feel special. As a result, her business has earned a great reputation locally, her business continues to grow by word of mouth, and she doesn't fall victim to the seasonality many other businesses do.

The second key for Cookie was having a detailed, written business plan. She spent two years developing her plan and doing all the research before she even opened the business. She still uses that plan to this day. She says it allows her to stay on track and not be distracted by trendy ideas that may work, if only for a short time, for others. After her first full year in business, Cookie did something especially interesting. She put her business' actual financial numbers back into her business plan and after running the math found they were extremely close to the forecast numbers she put together in the original plan. Given that most people starting a business will exaggerate those numbers to make them look good for whoever is reviewing the plan, Cookie's accuracy is all the more impressive.

So, what does this mean to you? We sincerely hope it means you see the value in having a written and detailed business plan. Moreover, it is important to run your business from that plan and not to stuff it in a binder to be forgotten for a decade. A business plan should be a living document and not a tool to secure financing or some short-term business goal. Rather, it should be a guide and accountability tool that you reflect on constantly. Below is a partial list of what a detailed business plan can do for you:

1. How to prepare for change and assess and mitigate potential risks

2. How to capitalize on opportunities and overcome business challenges

3. How to conduct/assess competitor analysis

4. How to define and act on a niche market

By now, we believe you see many benefits to having a business plan, but we hope you also see the significant value in having one for yourself and your business. We want you to run your business from a plan, have regular check-ins for accountability, and use the business plan like a compass to chart your course.

If you don't feel you have the experience or expertise to do one on your own or you want an objective opinion and approach, then get help. There are lots of excellent organizations, businesses, coaches, and consultants specializing in this area who can help – CAP Leadership Solutions and the HOP Performance Institute are, humbly, two of many great options. Of equal importance is having a coach, mentor, or peer advisory group to help keep you accountable to your goals. This individual or group will care about your success and will be an integral part of your team.

Believe

What does it mean to believe? Donald Davidson talks about concepts, belief, and language. What do you believe? What is a belief? Donald Davidson believes that thinking is built from different human emotions such "as belief, desire, intention, intentional action, memory, perception, and all the rest of attitudes and attributes"[5] Our thought processes start from a certain belief which leads to the next belief.

Earlier we talked about the value of a vision that inspires. We believe if you are reading this book you have a dream and a vision for the future you dream of so we say "Go Get It!"

---

[5] Davidson, Donald. "Rational Animals." In Subjective, Intersubjective, Objective, 96-106. New York: Oxford University Press (2001): 124).

We love the quote from the movie "Pursuit of Happyness" starring Will Smith. Smith's character (based on the true story of a man named Christopher Gardner) says to his son:

"Hey. Don't ever let somebody tell you... You can't do something. Not even me. All right? ... You got a dream... You gotta protect it. People can't do somethin' themselves, they wanna tell you you can't do it. If you want somethin', go get it. Period."

As you can imagine, Wai, like the rest of us, will get anxious and even scared initially at the thought of this. Fear is that evolutionary response humans have meant to keep us alive. However, we encourage you to be a dream maker and not a dream killer. Our advice to you when it comes time for you to take that first big step out of your own comfort zone – embrace the dream, don't run from it!

Fear can be crippling for most of us, but it doesn't need to be. So, how do you step up, move past the fear, and go to those heights you aspire? It's simple: do the things others aren't willing to do.

Whether you're a leader, a team member, or a candidate, success comes from having the discipline to do the things that you know you should be doing, even when you don't feel like doing them. When you practice this kind of self-discipline regularly, you'll naturally stand out from the pack—because most people avoid the hard stuff. It's just easier to put it off.

The truth is, however, what feels easy now creates problems down the line. And what feels hard now—doing the stuff you don't feel like—makes everything easier in the long-term. Self-discipline doesn't have to be hard—you just have to change the way you think about it.

Successful people have mastered the art of self-discipline. Corey has spent the last 10 years studying and coaching some of the most successful people in business, figuring out what makes them different. They're not smarter or more talented than the average person—they just consistently do what others aren't willing to do by keeping three principles in mind:

- Do it scared.
- Habits, not results.
- Remember the big picture.

Do it scared.

Fear is one of the biggest saboteurs of our goals, because it inhibits action. The next time you feel yourself putting something off because you're afraid—of uncertainty or failure—just "do it scared."

We heard a true story of a woman who was trapped in a burning building on the 80th floor. She was terrified of heights and enclosed spaces, and when the fire alarm went off, she refused to follow her colleagues into the stairwell to evacuate to safety. The firemen did a sweep of the building and found her hiding under her desk, waiting to die. She was screaming "I'm scared! I'm scared!" as the firemen tried to get her to walk down the stairwell until one fireman said, "That's OK, just do it scared." He repeated it all the way down the 80 flights of stairs, until he brought her to safety.

We've all faced these moments in our careers—when you know what needs to be done, but your fear holds you back. In order to stand out, you must develop the habit of acting in the face of fear. It's fine to be scared—do it scared. It's fine to be unsure—do it unsure. It's fine to be uncomfortable—do it uncomfortable. Just do something.

This is the attitude of the most disciplined and successful people on the planet. They might be scared, but they do it anyway. And by just doing something, you create movement - generating momentum that will lead to progress and results.

Habits, not results.

Perfectionism is one of the most common reasons people procrastinate, and we've all done it at some point.

The best way to overcome this impulse is to put your self-esteem into stellar work habits instead of results. It can take a while to see the fruits of your labour—whether you're spearheading a new initiative, trying to launch a business, or planning a second career. To keep yourself motivated, take pride in sticking to your work habits, rather than looking for immediate results. In time, success will follow.

Remember the big picture.

During the pursuit of any goal, we will inevitably encounter obstacles. The difference between those who stand out in their careers and those who blend in lies in what you do when you reach these critical turning points. Do you hesitate and turn back? Or do you press forward? When you feel frustrated, depressed, or disappointed, don't give up—just get some perspective.

Stop fixating on the here and now and think about the big picture. Today's challenges may not make sense, but you must have faith that over the long term, they will be nothing more than minor blips on your radar screen.

Having this perspective and faith will help you press forward at the moments when others turn back.

Contrary to popular belief, people who have reached the highest levels in their careers aren't necessarily better educated, more talented, or better connected. Neither are they simply more motivated or harder workers. Rather, successful people have realized that getting to the top means that they first have to do the things they don't want to do.

It's not about enjoying self-discipline—it's about adopting a few new ways of thinking that simply make discipline easier to endure. And when you develop the habit of doing things that others won't, you're putting yourself on the fast track to the top.

Thanks to Drago Adams for his contribution to the content of this chapter.

Change

> *"Be the change that you wish to see in the world."*
> *(Mahatma Gandhi)*

Nothing stays the same. Everything is always changing, including us. We recognize it's hard to do something new because we have never done it before, but change can be freeing and sometimes we feel a lot of freedom with even a small change. That said, most of us don't want to change if we don't have to.

This is Wai's take on change:

> *"Two powerful words that helped me come out of the dark and into the light were enough and more. I worked on eliminating the word enough*

and reaching for more in my life. The difference in my life after becoming conscious of these words as you can see has been very enlightening and rewarding.

"Do you want to change your life, or do you want to stay just where you are?

"This very question motivated me to change. Keep in mind the only person you can change is you! Stop trying to change everyone around you. Stop complaining about circumstances. Making people and things as you would like them comes after your personal change.

"The key is to accept that only you have the ability to change."

In order to affect change, we are required to stop preserving the status quo. The following is a great tidbit[6]: "Entrepreneurs are rebels with tremendous courage and passion. Our question to you is: 'What are you going to do to be A Positive Rebel?'"

Machiavelli himself stated: *"I'm not interested in preserving the status quo; I want to overthrow it."* The entrepreneur/achiever should have at least a bit of the rebel inside. Being interested in, or, worse yet, content with the status quo, is counterculture for achievers. Given the era in which he lived, Machiavelli has some great quotes, particularly when it comes to the subject of ruling and strategizing to move into leadership. The concept of overthrowing the status quo has a visceral appeal to most every entrepreneur and achiever we know.

---

[6] http://www.companyfounder.com/2011/01/dont-preserve-the-status-quo/

Maintain the entrepreneurial, rebel spirit in everything you do.

Once you embrace the idea of change you will require resilience. So, what is resilience and how can you build it? Educational consultant, speaker and author, Ray Mathis of Mental and Emotional Karate discusses what it means to be resilient, why some are resilient while others aren't, and how anyone can learn to be resilient[7].

We often define resilience as "bounce back ability." Some other definitions of resilience we found in dictionaries include the words: springing back; returning to original shape or form after being bent, stretched, compressed; buoyant; cheerful. We like these because people talk about being "all bent out of shape", "stretched to their limits", "under a lot of pressure", and how "I'm keeping

---

[7] http://www.mentalandemotionalkarate.com/

my head above water". Resilience is how people manage and recover from these situations.

The trouble many people have, however, is they generate more emotion than is necessary or helpful in these contexts. They experience more emotion than they want, certainly more than they know what to do with, and they get stuck there. The more emotion we generate, the more reactive and less resilient we become. Emotional overwhelm causes people to make mistakes therefore, by extension, making their and others' lives worse.

The following formula explains why they do that:

EVENT + THOUGHTS = FEELINGS [which leads to] > BEHAVIOUR.

Thoughts cause feelings, not events, and behavior tends to follow our emotions toward our life events. There is always more than one way to look at anything that happens to us. Some ways make us feel better, others worse. Some make it easier to deal with life events, others harder.

Being resilient means generating enough energy to do what we need to do in a given situation, but not so much that we overreact to it and generate all those negative emotions.

We all create cognitive and emotional ruts from practicing thinking and feeling the same ways. Once we make these ruts, we can't get rid of them. However, we can make new ones for thinking or looking at things in more helpful ways, ways that allow us to generate a more functional amount of emotion, and to spring back, return to our original shape or form after being bent, stretched or compressed – which allows us to "keep our heads above water" and remain cheerful.

Others can often provide us with more helpful ways of looking at things, but we need to put in the practice to make these new ways as automatic as our old ways were. But know it's also normal to slip back into our old ways from time to time, even after diligently practicing new ways. It's part of being human.

Another post Corey did was titled "Eeyore or Owl - Your Choice" In the article he says:

Obstacles inspire creativity and innovation and can be a motivator if you choose to embrace them!

Carol Dweck brings insight into how a growth mindset views and approaches challenges as learning opportunities. Research by Angela Duckworth on grit shows we need passion and perseverance towards long-term goals. We know research exists on dispositional optimism (please check that out...it is not 'Polyanna' thinking but rather choosing to look for some positives in all circumstances to paraphrase and oversimplify the concept). At a common-sense level, I believe we all want to see, hear and feel, people who are interested in solutions versus "just talking or complaining about obstacles and challenges or present circumstance." Today, Simon Sinek shared this quote: "When we point to obstacles, we inhibit progress. When we offer solutions, we advance it." What are you doing today, this week, this month, this year to advance progress? Challenges and setbacks will happen on the path and progress to excellence so get over the negative feelings when it happens as quick as possible to get your mindset reset to solutions and learning that keep you moving forward and learning. Rather than complaining about results or

circumstance learn from it and get creative, inspired, and re-energized and motivated to move towards progress and solution as you continue to better yourself daily.

My challenge to all of you: Embrace challenges and obstacles and look at them as opportunities to grow and learn. Do not give up too easy or too quick like the herd of the masses. you were created to be exceptional and deserve to embrace that potential. To use the Winnie the Pooh Metaphor - "Don't be the Eeyore (everything is negative) in the room, be the Tigger (energy) or the wise owl everyone goes to for wisdom or guidance."

Have you found your calling yet? Often that question, or more accurately the answer to it, is the trigger for change in our lives. This leads us back to the Gandhi quote: "Be the change that you wish to see in the world."

Corey did a blog post in March 2018 titled "Be The Change: A New Measure of ROI." In the post he talks about insights he got from his friend Shannon Graham. Here is that post:

I heard a great insight today from my new friend, and premier motivational speaker and leader in the self-help and coaching industry, Shannon Graham in Santa Barbara, CA. He talks of no longer selling just his knowledge but instead using his 'gift' (in his case his creativity) to help clients answer questions where the answer does not exist. This shifted his level of value higher in his clients lives as well as his own. He encourages people to do the type of work which you enjoy and what you truly desire. Two benefits to this: 1. You add more value to your clients.; 2. You add more value to yourself as you continue to grow and create impact.

Too many leaders reach a value of development that they feel is good enough, and that might be even higher than they ever dreamed to begin with. However, I say you want to think of those you serve first and the contribution you have for the world - your calling. Focusing on your calling pulls us into "Higher Order Performance" and living into our essence (from Steve Miller of Implicit Solutions and his Implicit Career Search). Joseph Campbell calls this "the hero's journey." We have so much more potential than our minds can ever imagine. Science has proven this and great thought leaders throughout history dating back thousands of years speak of this. It takes tapping into things at a higher order level, an unconscious level and some may say even a spiritual level of our being, to bring a conscious awareness to "what if" possibilities.

Shannon's encouragement is to live forward into what you want. Get super clear on what that is and then, as Nike puts it, just do it! The golden nugget he leaves people within his Facebook video was the affect of that is that not only does it helps clients along with yourself, but it creates a tremendous ROI - RIPPLE OF IMPACT. Ultimately, this ROI creates something that is exponentially better than anything you are currently doing.

Brian Johnson from Optimize talks of Areté. Guys like Socrates, Plato and Aristotle said that if you want happiness you better live with Areté—a word that literally means virtue or excellence but has a deeper meaning, something closer to "living at your highest potential moment to moment to moment."

Simon Sinek says *"A boss tells people what they can do to achieve a goal. A leader asks people what they can do to advance a vision."* Linking this with ROI I will put it this way: "A boss tells people what they can do to achieve a goal focused on financial ROI - Return on Investment." This is the standard model of performance that creates incremental performance improvements. However, "A leader asks people what they can do to advance a vision and focuses on ROI - Ripple of Impact." This creates purpose and meaningfulness for all and leads to greater significance for all stakeholders. It is both inward and outward focused. This is team building and changing the world type of impact. Like a small drop of water in the ocean changes the make up of the entire ocean forever, so too does your ROI – Ripple of Impact. Go forward and create the impact you are meant and built for!

Choices

Wai has succeeded in producing his own unique and thought-provoking study of what makes Wai run! What makes him tick is facing up to the challenges of life and choosing to master them rather than to let them beat him down. The simple language in which he states this conviction is its own eloquence.

From a profound depression in which he felt helpless to defeat the twin scourges of multiple sclerosis and cerebral palsy he has developed a positive philosophy by which he has changed from being helpless to getting more from life. It becomes a matter of risk: "…as you take more risk, you will fail from time to time, but your failures will lead to success, and you will live life fully."

Wai's enthusiasm for whatever he's doing is contagious. He's tried making music videos, doing promotions, and even tried to become a painter. He's never suffered from a lack of projects, or "ideas" as he calls them, and has stumbled more than once in his struggle for recognition, but every time he picks himself up, he becomes shrewder and wiser. As he says: "You have the power to choose the kind of energy that you wish to attract into your life. Positive energy is the result of positive thoughts. You have the power to choose."

How are you choosing to use your gift?

We make choices everyday. One choice we make is how and with whom we are going to create positive impact. We want to have the greatest amount of impact combined with influence and inspiration. This is because what we do for others has a direct impact on how we feel about ourselves.

To make choices that have this level of purpose and meaningfulness, we first need to be aware of the choices we make and that we have far more control over choices and what happens in our lives than we think. Next, we need to become more aware of the beliefs and attitudes behind these choices as they shape our feelings and thoughts. Corey heard from his good friend Steve Miller of Implicit Solutions refer to this as "the story we tell ourselves". When we make choices driven from the essence of who we are - the REAL us, not a role or identity we create - we feel congruency and that is when the three "Is" kick in (Influence, Impact, and Inspiration).

The opposite is true as well. When we make choices based on who we think people want us to be or play into a role or story we created that is not connected to who we really are to our core then we feel "Dis-Content". We are disconnected to and experience no contentment in those choices. We may even feel like a sell out.

Joseph Campbell talks of "The Hero's Journey[8]. and that we all have a

---

[8] " Campbell, Joseph, Cousineau, Phil, and Brown, Stuart L. The Hero's Journey : The World of Joseph Campbell : Joseph Campbell on His Life and Work. 1st ed. San Francisco: Harper & Row, 1990. Print

contribution to make to this world. We believe that is our essence. Indigenous peoples would go on vision quests to find their essence. Many today go on spiritual journeys or quests. Whatever you do, it's important to connect to your essence and have it as the core filter for prioritizing in your life. This way, you can make the right choices to make you feel your best and create maximum positive impact.

Corey says this:

"I do know that a big part of it for me was realizing when I connected to my essence and purpose, as much as it is mine and what I feel "called to do", it is bigger than me and it is about my gift to the world - my contribution. A contribution is a gift. How are you choosing to use your gift?"

Maybe you're unsure on what that gift is and there are many ways to help connect to that. Realize we all have a contribution to make and that contribution impacts others and ultimately makes us feel better about ourselves.

Being Responsible

Wai often talks about coming from the old school of thinking – "If you don't work, you don't eat." We think too many young adults have had a soft life. They're at risk of being unwilling to be emotionally tough as society has created and supported structures that discourage competition and struggle. We give medals to or reward anyone who just signs up for a competition. Our question is this: How will they live in the real world that will present them with obstacles, challenges, and competition if we don't allow them to develop resilience when they are young?

The only way for a person to get stronger and better is to deal with the challenges that the world gives you. Good or bad, they are all important lessons. Wai is the first to admit he didn't believe this statement 20 years ago. He says, "Believe me, it's been a difficult journey, but because of that I am now living my dream."

If you're facing a challenge and anxious about your situation, we know how you feel. All three of us, as of the writing of this book, have recently been or are going through major health, financial, or business crises. Just this year, Wai had a heart attack, we have family members battling cancer, and yet we know we need to battle through the adversity. We are in this race called life and it's a marathon, not a sprint. We have one thing we can all be responsible for and that is the attitude we choose in light of some challenging circumstances.

Whether it is the day Wai was in the hospital after his heart attack, Corey having to shut down a college and deal with the personal financial loss, or Kirk looking after his wife following breast cancer surgery and chemotherapy, we all thought it was a terrible event in our lives. It sounds bad. It felt bad. At the time, it was bad.

However, we decided we wouldn't let these challenges take us down. That's when we knew we had to change what we were thinking and doing. Like many challenges people face, it led to a deeper discovery and enhanced clarity on our life's mission and purpose. What we chose to focus on was that the worst event in our life could be a trigger for something far greater in the future – something we may not have moved toward had these negative events not happened.

We are not alone.

Gallup did a study and asked people to identify the worst and best event of their life. They found that there was an 80% correlation between the two events – their life's worst event was also their greatest.[9]

Many studies have been done through the years on people who seem to define success. They seemed to have it all; wealth, success, great relationships, etc. The researchers were surprised to discover that every one of these "charmed" people had bad things happen to them. They all experienced challenges and adversity, however, each one of them turned the bad into good and their misfortune into fortune.

Challenges and change are a part of life. The waves of change are always coming our way, but when the wave hits, we have a choice. We can embrace it and ride it to a successful future or resist it - and get crushed.

---

[9] https://news.gallup.com

Embracing those waves of challenge and change is all about how we perceive and respond to the events we face. In the Sunday, March 29, 2015 edition of Monday Morning Motivator Newsletter titled "The Shark and the Goldfish," Drago Adams shares the positive success formula below:

E + P = O

We can't always control the (E)vents in our life but we can control our (P)ositive response to these events and this often determines the (O)utcome. When the change hits, instead of focusing on the challenge we can choose to look for the opportunity. We can ask what this event is teaching us and identify how we can grow stronger and wiser from it. We can live in fear or move forward with faith and take positive action.

We can decide to be a shark instead of a goldfish. Goldfish are limited by fear. They stay in their comfort zone and wait for someone to feed them. On the other hand, sharks (nice sharks, that is) move forward with faith and take action. They trust that their best days are ahead of them, not behind them. Instead of waiting to be fed they venture into the ocean of possibility in search of food. Their beliefs and actions create a self-filling prophecy; because they expect to find food and take action to find it, they do.

Shark or goldfish? Which will you choose to be?

Commitment to Excellence

When looking at commitment, specifically a commitment to excellence, Wai has the following insights. When he commits to projects intended to serve others and better the world, he says:

"At that moment I realize that it's too late for me to back out of these projects – I have people counting on me and supporting me. I have lots going on. I'm swimming 40 laps and writing a book about it to raise funds for the YMCA Women's Shelter while at the same time promoting my speeches, books, and workshops about motivation. Anyone can write motivational books or speeches, but if I can show people how motivation works, then people may become more inspired by seeing me swim and how I've pulled everything together. People can see it's working for me and they'll understand what I'm writing about in my books."

From our (Corey and Kirk's) perspective, as we work with organizations, teams, and businesses looking for elite-level performance, we continue to learn a lot about what's needed in the commitment to excellence - reaching the elite-level ideal. We begin by asking the not-so-small question: What is the ultimate potential of your leadership? This is driven by the burning question Corey had as a child: Can average people, from average circumstances, achieve elite or world-class performance?

In your leadership struggles, you may have asked yourself:

Am I (Are we) reaching our potential as a company (organization/team)?

What's wrong? Everyone tells me I am successful, but the truth is that I am unhappy and feel unfulfilled.

How do I get exponential (breakthrough) performance rather than only incremental performance?

How can I overcome high turnover, absenteeism, and other current workplace issues?

Will I ever get out of this rut, have balance, and be rewarded for all this hard work?

How can I get more efficiencies and make more profits?

How do I get my team more motivated?

How do I get a performance culture?

Will I ever be able to retire or exit my business?

How can I connect to the drivers of exponential performance?

Asking those kinds of questions is fantastic! That means you know there's something more out there and you're looking for ways to remain committed to your own excellence.

Even if you are enjoying some level of success you will likely find yourself wondering what more you can do or accomplish and how this can positively impact the world while also finding a deeper sense of purpose. No one on their deathbed regrets taking risks and trying something with worthy intent, but they will regret those times they chose not to move towards their dreams and "What If…" potential.

The vision for your business or organization is likely one of a performance culture and motivated teams; though your reality may be closer to one that features high turnover, absenteeism, burnout, declining profits, lacking innovation and a constant stream of workplace issues. Overwhelmed by day-to-day struggles, you've lost sight of your vision and greater purpose. You're spending more time working in the business than on the business, and the incremental growth isn't adding up to the exponential potential you know is possible. You need to be responsible, make better decisions, and get passionate to move into your calling and the potential locked inside you!

Audience pain/problem or unrealized passion/potential:

1.   Desire high growth and breakthrough (exponential type growth) and want to create a high performing team through strong leadership

2.   Pain Point: a) Stuck and need tools to get unstuck, b) Working too much and too hard for results and feel no balance in their life, c) They are successful but feel something is missing (and they aren't happy-/satisfied)

If getting to the elite level means getting into the top 1% how do you do it? How do you differentiate when every product or service can be commodified? What you have is incremental growth; what you want is exponential growth.

What you want is substantial growth, though you need to get beyond the struggles, stagnation and the shit that keeps hitting the fan in the day-to-day business.

You need systems that enable you to get your head above the clouds and see the big picture of your business to move it forward. Clarity is everything, because there can be no progression when you are focused on fear and operating in reactionary mode.

Something is missing, and it's leading to ever-increasing unhappiness and unfulfillment for you and those in the organization. We have all heard stories of people who seem to have it all, the financial success, top health and athletic performance, lots of toys and stuff but are never happy or have the relationships around them suffering and falling apart. The feel no matter what they get or accomplish there is always a void or emptiness. The achievements and results and stuff and everything money can buy can't bring that deeper sense of spiritual level fulfillment and happiness of a life well lived and contributions that speak to a life that create impact for others.

Here is what we know.

Staying at the current state (Point A) can lead to:

- the focus being on performance (money, primarily, which is a result, not a driver) – not drivers of performance

- focussing on numbers and money only and lacking purpose and meaningfulness. Teams are unmotivated and don't buy in (or trust) the organization and the goals being set regarding performance

- being leader- and organization-centric, not team-oriented and motivating which is truly what leads to high performance. Leaders do very little of the performance delivery they are measuring and demanding.

- not being sure how to measure performance and create high-performance cultures. (The relativity of success, risk of complacency, and staying in a comfort zone because things are going well). This mindset misses the potential within and the growth, learning and rewards for all that come with that.

- Performance trap mindset – untapped potential

- Operate on fear and are always in reactionary mode vs. strategic, proactive, optimistic, deliberate, challenging, and rewarding

- Not asking the right questions – (i.e. instead of how to get 5 to 10 % growth next year based on $10 Million in sales/profit last year)– Ask: are we actually a $10 M dollar company? Or are we a $100 M dollar company that hasn't moved into our potential yet? What opportunities exist to help us move into a stronger reality (What will drive growth – Opportunities MEETS Drivers of Performance)

- Sabotage of leader and the goals by the team

- High turnover, absenteeism, burnout, declining clients and profits, declining innovation, and creativity

How can you realize a breakthrough of exponential performance that fosters well-being for your team and a better work-life balance for you? Can you imagine creating a business or career that functions smoothly and creates purpose and meaning for you and the team and clients you serve? Imagine all the financial freedom of never worrying about money ever again and being able to give of your time and money freely while knowing your family and generations to come are set up and secure. Imagine doing more of the things you love to do and delegating or no longer doing those things you dislike doing. Everything you do flows with fun and ease and money and impact seems to be attracted to you. This is the ideal.

There are two reasons why not all people achieve success: they give up too easily or they give up too quickly. Most organizations and teams focus on goals and growth with incremental performance every year, but few look to the drivers of performance that can provide breakthrough performance. Getting into the top 1% of business requires an equal focus on all aspects of organizational life: purpose and vision, mindset, grit, planning, team-building, conflict resolution, internal and external relationship building, employee and client retention, deliberate practice, and improved decision making.

The ideal state (Point B) and the results:

- Steady and sustainable results that flow with fun and ease.
- Financial abundance, security, and flexibility.
- Creating meaning and purpose for yourself and others while improving the human condition.
- Continual learning and development opportunities for you, your team, and your loved ones.

- A motivated performance culture that everyone is attracted to, buys into, and consistently achieves the objectives of the team.
- Opportunities for growth are continually present to you and you're able to capitalize on the ones that make sense and deliver the greatest impact.
- Happier, higher-performing, cohesive teams with high engagement and a strong sense of well-being.
- Their "Why" - their purpose, their contribution to the world - is crystal clear!
- Knowing that what you measure is important and that you're improving the drivers of performance, happiness, and meaning
- Having the time and financial flexibility to do what you want, when you want, and with whom you want.

How you are going to take them from Point A to Point B?

We run a number of programs through the HOP® Performance Institute and CAP Leadership Solutions, but the best way to answer the question above is to talk to what we do personally. Below is what we aim to do in our lives and through our businesses. Our mission:

To improve lives of the less fortunate in the world through education, leadership, and entrepreneurship so that they can live better lives and have better opportunities in the future.

One particular way we aim to achieve our mission is through the school a year campaign. Our goal is to help build a school a year in parts of the world where people who would not normally have the opportunity to go to school would be given the opportunity. Through this we provide infrastructure. However, to ensure this is sustainable and ongoing costs for running the school are maintained we do so through social enterprise. For instance, we may set up a sewing centre for the parents of the children coming to the school and provide opportunities to learn a trade (textiles and tailoring) that helps pay for the school costs for the children as well as meals for the child as well as the adult working in the sewing centre. Further, the working learns a trade and may be able to get work outside the sewing centre through a local tailor of retail outlet and this provides additional income for the household that could lead to improvement in housing or living conditions. Even more than improving the socio-economic circumstance of those that are served through our mission, we are changing the mindset and bringing hope and giving the story that those positively affected can use to help others embrace the "what if" potential and opportunities available in the world.

It also teaches a "hand-up" approach versus "handout" which very rarely works or is sustainable long term. Moreover, our clients, instructors, and team have the opportunity to get involved in meaningful and impactful projects locally and worldwide and we find this changes their hearts and gratitude and leads to them wanting to do more and create ROI –a "Ripple of Impact."

Wai is constantly looking for organizations and individuals who he can help through his fundraising events. He hopes his inspiration and example encourage others to get engage and get them to commit to excellence – in achievements but also impact.

So, what are you going to do to create your own ROI – Ripple of Impact!

Grit

"Nothing in this world can take the place of persistence. Talent will not; nothing is more common than unsuccessful men with talent. Genius will not; unrewarded genius is almost a proverb. Education will not; the world is full of educated derelicts. Persistence and determination alone are omnipotent. The slogan 'Press On' has solved and always will solve the problems of the human race."

— *Calvin Coolidge*

Wai would not be where he is today if it were not for the persistence and determination of his mother as well as his own perseverance to overcome obstacles and challenges. Like Wai, we can choose to be victim or a victor. Most of us would choose a victor if asked, but our behaviour, attitude, and language can make us act, think, and sound like a victim. This can be as simple as complaining when things don't go our way, feeling it isn't worth the effort to even try, or we just feel comfortable with how things are versus how great we want them to be. There's a big difference between being complacent or comfortable and being grateful for the life we have. We can experience gratitude simultaneously with the desire to want more out of life for ourselves and others. This is how Wai lives his life. Does he live his life this way 100% of the time? Heck, no. He's human, too.

The difference is something academics have called "dispositional optimism" which basically is seeing the positives in things versus the negatives. This is not "Pollyanna thinking" – believing everything is wonderful all the time. Rather, it's finding the good in your circumstances and choosing to focus on the positive aspects. This is difficult for all of us and requires – grit.

Angela Duckworth from the University of Pennsylvania is the foremost authority on grit. She defines grit simply as passion and persistence for long-term goals, or expressed mathematically:

GRIT = Passion + Persistence + Long-term Goals

We believe there are other character traits which factor into someone's grit:

"Guts" – personal courage and determination; toughness of character
Perseverance – to achieve despite difficulties, failure, or opposition
Tenacity – being very determined

Fortitude – courage in pain or adversity
Resilience – recovering positively from setbacks
"Stick-to-it-iveness"

Fortunately, the qualities that combine to create grit are teachable and learnable. Therefore, anyone can improve their level of grit. Grit is not based on IQ. Grit is as essential as talent to high achievement. Life will throw us curveballs, provide challenges, and throw up obstacles. Any level of success that is sustainable and meaningful requires effort. In fact, in Duckworth says, "effort counts twice" when it comes to being gritty. Below is an explanation of the role of effort in acquiring world-class achievements:

Coaching + Practice > Talent
Effort counts twice:
Talent + Effort = Skill
Skill + Effort = Achievement

Now you're asking yourself: "How do I get gritty?" Well, having an intrinsic, deep-rooted interest in the "thing" requiring grit is an excellent starting point. Enjoyment of the activity/job/task makes it easier to be grittier! Another element that helps build grit are concepts we wrote about earlier in the book – purpose and meaning. Add a little bit of both and watch your grit meter rise. Sprinkle in some "deliberate practice" supported by coaches and other support mechanisms, mix with equal parts of resolve and resilience, and your grit will be well on its way to where you want it to be.

The positive habits you'll need to have include:

Reflective or "mental toughness"
Resiliency
Persistence
Dispositional optimism: creativity and reframing

Courage
Patience
Hope
Vision

Here is where the HOP® Model talks of wellbeing and the need to use HERO.

Wellbeing = Hope + Efficacy + Resiliency + Optimism (HERO)

When trying to figure out why not all people achieve success, we found two key factors: they give up too easily and they give up too quickly.

Corey has studied grit extensively in his PhD studies and has used the Grit 12 questionnaire is some of his own research. The questionnaire is twelve questions that when answered give you a baseline grit score. When you work on improving grit you can answer those questions again to see if your grit has improved. The questionnaire points to either drivers or saboteurs of grit which give those who take it an indication of areas to work on if they want to either improve their overall grit or become more aware of what is holding them back.

A big part of grit is simply not giving up. Our greatest weakness lives in giving up. The most certain way to success is trying one more time.

Failure is no biggie. Just ask Thomas Edison. If he stopped at failure, he wouldn't have moved on to invent a little thing called the light bulb. Or the phonograph. Or the motion picture camera. We pretty much owe Edison for movies, music and lights. Thank goodness he pressed on and didn't give up!

Young Edison only had three months of traditional schooling. Not because he was brilliant, but because his mind often wandered, and his teacher thought him to be "addled." His unique path to learning came from his mother, who schooled him at home and nursed him through what ended up being lifelong hearing problems. Despite the challenges, he went on to change the world.

What's stopping you from your dream? Maybe you failed a class somewhere else. Or a scheduling conflict is messing with your plans. Turn that setback, challenge, or obstacle into the motivation you need to move past it and to live the potential you are meant to fulfill and called to.

Below are some questions and exercises you can review and ask yourself to improve grit in your life:

Explain how developing grit can change your approach to life? Explain whether or not you believe you can raise your grit score and why?

Write a short three-paragraph essay on someone you know who is "gritty." Think about the setbacks that didn't prevent them from achieving their goal.

Challenge

Let's think back to Wai's early life: growing up in Hong Kong in an environment toward people with disabilities; moving to a new country at a young age; having to learn a second language while being the new kid at school; having a disability; having a speech impediment. Those are enough challenges all on their own.

So why does Wai continue to take on additional challenges? It's because he loves to challenge himself to go the distance.

Wai told us this story when writing this book.

> *"Most of my life, I have had mental challenges in writing essays at school. I write papers that are 2000-3000 words. I have written three motivational*

books. Despite my physical challenges, I rode a horse for ten hours one day in the Kamloops Cattle Drive in 1994. My body hurt all over. I did nothing but sit on the horse. Now I am in the pool about two and a half hours and I swim 34 laps with one good arm and the other arm and legs do not work well. Please do not feel sorry for me, because it would not help me a bit. This is my choice. I want to explore the human spirit. I would like to know how far a person can push himself to his limit. What kind of a person is he? One should always test oneself for the greatness in one. We will be surprised with what we will find in ourselves.

"I truly realize now I must use the things that I have learned

from others who have entered my life, others who taught me things to make my life better. When they have to leave me to help others, I should not be sad, instead I should be happy that we had the time together. We were able to be in each other's lives and learn from each other. I believe each person who enters our lives has a purpose. When the time is up, we should let them go and make room for the next person that enters our life. I think our lives are rich because we can learn from others. Nothing will last forever. I have to take what I learnt from them and try to make my life better than before I met them, because it is the only way for me to honour them for the time they have given me."

Drago Adam, in his Monday Motivator, wrote the following article on 13 Challenges to Pursue:

1. Review your performance.
Whether it's your communication skills, whether it's recent activity, whether it's as a CEO or whether it's on the job. Here's what my father said: "Always do more than you are paid for to make an investment in your future."

2. Face your fears.
That's how you conquer them. Don't dismiss them—face them.

3. Exercise your willpower to change direction.
You don't have to keep doing what you've been doing the last six years if it's not yielding the benefits you want. Pick a new destination and go that way. Use your willpower to start the process. Clean up the errors. Invest it

now in the next year. Watch it make the difference.

4. Admit your mistakes.
Sometimes you have to admit them to others. One of the best phrases in the English language? "I'm sorry." (Humble Pie may taste bad. but it's good for the soul)

5. Refine your goals.
Set some higher goals. Go for something beyond what you thought you could do.

6. Believe in yourself.
You've got to believe in the possibilities. There isn't a skill you can't learn; there isn't a discipline you can't try; there isn't a class you can't take; there isn't a book you can't read.

7. Ask for wisdom.
This is communication of the highest source. Ask for wisdom that creates answers. Ask for the wisdom that creates faith to believe things are

possible. Don't wish it was easier; wish you were better.

8. Invest your profits.
Profits are better than wages. Wages make you a living; profits make you a fortune.

9. Live with intensity.
You might as well turn it up a notch or two. Invest more of you in whatever you do. Be a little stronger; be a little wiser. Step up your vitality contribution. Put everything you've got into everything you do and then ask for more vitality, more strength and more vigor, more heart and more soul.

10. Find your place.
If you just work on a job, find the best place you can serve well, and sure enough they'll ask you to occupy a better place. Keep doing your job well; do the very best you can. That's your best way out.

11. Demand integrity from yourself.
Integrity is like loyalty. You can't
demand it of someone else; you can
only demand it of yourself. Be the best
example of loyalty, and you'll get
some loyal followers. Be the best
example of integrity, and you'll have
people around you who have
integrity. Lead the way.

12. Welcome the disciplines.
Disciplines build cities. A well-
disciplined activity creates
abundance, creates uniqueness,
creates productivity.

13. Fight for what's right.
If you want something valuable,
you've got to fight for it. Fight the
enemy and keep faith. Fight the illness
and keep faith. Fight the evil and keep
faith. We trust you all are up to the
challenge to become the best you can
be and remember to celebrate the
little victories along the way!

Within challenges comes the opportunity to test our mental capacity and stamina. In Corey's research, he found that one of the best ways to embrace challenges and obstacles is through what is called "dispositional optimism." One might say it's like looking at the bright side of things versus the bad. This is not Pollyanna thinking and rose-coloured glasses but rather looking for the positives and learning from and through challenges.

One thing has become very clear to us after having worked and talked with thousands of people and – at the risk of stating the obvious – that one thing is that people have good days and bad days. Some people have more good days than bad and vice-versa, but we all have both and we like to think that's a good thing. We celebrate the good days and how great we feel. We also acknowledge that we "aren't quite right" during those challenging days. Challenges give us opportunities to appreciate those good days that much more. Moreover, the challenging days are where character is built and honed.

Many of the world's greatest accomplishments were completed through periods of struggle or times of intense stress or pressure. Two examples to illustrate this point are India's independence and the U.S. civil rights movement. We also believe our focus determines our perception and, ultimately, our outcomes – a self fulfilling prophecy. When we focus on being mad, sad, or bitter, we directly, and negatively, influencing how we feel. We then find more excuses to support those feelings since that's where our focus lays, and we tend to see what we focus on. Alternatively, and more productively, we can choose to see the positives; we can choose to be happy, grateful, thinking abundantly, and about possibilities, therefore attracting those people and experience which will support that kind of life. This has often been called the Law of Attraction and many authors through history have talked or written about this.[10]

Corey was recently asked, during a time of significant transition along with its accompanying challenges, how things were going. Keeping in mind this concept of "dispositional optimism", Corey's answer went like this:

"I've realized that no matter where I go and what circumstance I'm in, I figure 90% of the time it's great and 10% of the time it sucks, but I have a choice on which to focus on so I

---

[10] https://thelawofattraction.org/law-of-attraction-authors/

choose the 90%." I've been thinking of that a lot lately and realize focus can expand the good and minimize the bad. Allow yourself to have the odd bad day since sometimes circumstances make it the logical, reasonable, and appropriate thing to do (i.e. being sad over the loss of a loved one) but don't stay stuck there forever. I remember those feelings when I lost my dad and then my mother, but it was shortly after that I shifted to writing the eulogy that I got to focus on the positives and celebrate their lives with loved ones that helped get through those tough times. We know sometimes life happens, things aren't always fair, and not everyone is reasonable or shares the same values or integrity and we may have little control over certain aspects of our lives or situations, but we can choose our own attitudes and behaviours. I challenge all of you to choose the bright side!"

Growth Mindset

Now that you're familiar with grit, passion, and persistence for a long-term goal, we feel it's now important to give you a tool that helps you become "grittier." The best tool we have found is something Stanford Psychologist, Carol Dweck has termed "growth mindset" and it became extremely popular after her book Mindset: The New Psychology of Success came out in 2007. The Amazon write up for the book summarizes it well:

"In this brilliant book, Dweck shows how success in school, work, sports, the arts, and almost every area of human endeavor can be dramatically influenced by how we approach our goals. People with a fixed mindset—those who believe that abilities are fixed—are far less likely to flourish than those with a growth mindset—

those who believe that abilities can be developed through hard work, good strategies, and mentorship. Mindset reveals how great parents, teachers, managers, and athletes can put this idea to use to foster outstanding accomplishment."[11]

We want to add one other concept we believe is foundational to growth mindset, happiness, and growth in life and business - learning orientation. More specifically, when setting any performance or achievement goals we recommend having an accompanying and aligned learning goal. The learning that is needed, but also the learning that can happen if not successful in the timeline that was set at the outset, not only gives us a valuable tool for feedback and feedforward, it also helps us maintain our confidence and

---

[11] May 27, 2019 https://www.amazon.ca/Mindset-Psychology-Carol-S-Dweck/

efficacy. As far as learning orientation and growth mindset applies to goal setting, the best research we've come across is from Canadian researchers in a 2004 article in the Academy of Management Journal[12]. The general idea of the research is that it's more important to strive for learning than achievement. If you do this, the achievement and results will come.

Corey has come up with a word that he feels captures this thought: "PROFECTUS." We can use this and break it down:

> PRO - (Being paid as an expert in the field. Serious and highest level of sport, industry, or field. These people are at the elite level within and top 1 % in their field or on the path to

---

[12] Goal setting and goal orientation: An integration of two different yet related literatures. Seijts, G. H., Latham, G. P., Tasa, K., & Latham, B. W. (2004). Academy of Management Journal, 47(2), 227-239.

> getting into the top 1% and compensated for this expertise)
> FECT - Not going for perfect ... profect! Allows for continual learning and growth.
> US - Not just about you as "us" is a collective term

In striving to become an expert at the highest level in whatever it is you pursue or are passionate about the goal is continual learning and growth and that means none of us can do it on our own. All the greats throughout history had coaches, teachers, mentors, and embraced challenges and obstacles as opportunities for learning and developing their potential and move them towards the manifestation of their vision. Instead of waiting for the "perfect" idea we say go with a "profectus" idea and start! You will learn and develop, you will reach out to coaches, mentors, and teachers and others who can help you, and you will have the support and accountability needed to have not only the motivation but the drive to move into realizing your vision for your life and the impact you are called to.

The other benefit to leaders of taking a growth mindset and learning orientation with their teams is you will get a higher level of motivation within the team and greater "buy-in" for team and organizational goals. The learning provides the individuals on your team an intrinsic motivation that an externally delegated performance or achievement goal just can't provide.

Now, common sense leads us to the question: Why would anyone choose a fixed mindset and deterministic view of the world versus a growth mindset and having choice and removing those limitations? However, we all fall prey to some fixed mindset thoughts at times. So, a better question to ask is: "How do we get in the ZONE." The first step is awareness. Below is a tool that shows the difference between fixed mindset and growth mindset. This gives you awareness of when you are engaging in growth or fixed mindset. Further, the awareness of the growth mindset equivalent gives us an answer on how we can change our mindset from fixed to growth when we find we are stuck in a fixed mindset loop.

	FIXED MINDSET	**GROWTH MINDSET**
Intelligence	Static	Can be developed
Skills	Something you are born with	Come from hard work Can always be improved

Challenges	Something to avoid. Could reveal lack of skill. Tend to give up easily	Should be embraced An opportunity for growth. More persistent
Obstacles / Setbacks	Blame others Get discouraged	Use as wake-up call to work harder next time
Effort	Unnecessary Something you do when you aren't good enough	Essential A path to mastery
Criticism / Feedforward	Get defensive Take it personally	Useful Something to learn from Helps identify areas to improve
Success of Others	Comparison makes us "feel less than"	Celebrate others success Learn from

		others success
View of the World	Deterministic	Greater sense of free will and choice
Potential	Fixed	Unlimited and available through learning and embracing a "not yet" mindset

We know through our research that growth mindset drives motivation and achievement. We also know as we develop more of a growth mindset, we grow our level of gratitude which in turn opens up pathways to more opportunities and blessings.

Mindset > move to gratitude > open up pathways (opportunities/blessings)

How Do You Develop a Growth Mindset?[13]

Instead of…	**Try thinking…**
I'm not good at this.	What am I missing?
I give up.	I'll use a different strategy.
It's good enough.	Is this really my best work?
I can't make this any better.	I can always improve.
This is too hard.	This may take some time.
I made a mistake.	Mistakes help me learn.
I just can't do this.	I'm going to train my brain.
I'll never be that smart.	I'll learn how to do this.
Plan A didn't work.	There's always Plan B.

---

[13] https://medium.com/@veraliruiyu/how-to-develop-the-growth-mindset-8de56f47384d

My friend/colleague can do it.	I will learn from them.

Our final thoughts on this subject? Embrace a growth mindset and learning orientation and the power of "yet" as you move forward into your commitment to excellence and impact in this world. If it was not for looking at the challenges and obstacles that Wai has faced and faces daily as learning opportunities and a way to motivate him to action and to inspire others to do the same, life would be a lot tougher and a struggle. We are not saying that life will be without struggle and challenges with a growth mindset. However, challenges and struggles become easier to face and get past once you know the power of mindset and use challenges and obstacles for learning.

Power of our Words and Vocabulary

One of the workshops Corey and Kirk deliver is "The Language of Leadership." We encourage you to reflect on this question: How is your vocabulary?

Drago Adams wrote this in his weekly e-mail "The Monday Motivator" a few years back.

Sometimes the subtle difference in our attitude, which can make a major difference in our future, can be as simple as the language we use. It's the difference in even how you talk to yourself or others. It's consciously making a decision to quit saying what you don't want and to start saying what you do want. It's faith—believing in the best, hoping for the best and moving toward the best.

Instead of saying, "What if somebody doesn't respond?" start saying, "What if they do respond?" Instead of saying, "What if someone says no?" say, "What if they say yes?" Instead of saying, "What if they start and quit?" say, "What if they start and stay?" Instead of saying, "What if it doesn't work out?" say, "What if it does work out?"

When you start thinking and saying what you really want, then your mind automatically shifts and pulls you in that direction. And sometimes it can be that simple—just a little twist in vocabulary that illustrates your attitude and philosophy.

It is easy to stumble through almost a lifetime and not learn some of these simplicities. Then you have to put up with all the lack and all the challenges that don't work out simply from not reading the book, not listening to the lesson, not studying your language—not being willing to search so you can then find.

But here is the great news. You can start this process anytime. For me it was at age 25. At 25 I was broke. Six years later, I was a millionaire.

You might ask, "What kind of revolution, what kind of change, what kind of thinking, what kind of magic had to happen? Was it you?"

No.

Any person, any six years you go on an intensive, accelerated personal development curve, learning curve, application curve, you can learn the disciplines. Now, it might not take the same amount of time, but the same changes and the same rewards are available for those who pay that "six-year" price. And you might find that whether it's in the beginning to help get you started or in the middle to keep you on track, your language can have a great impact on your attitude, actions and results.[14]

The value of encouragement cannot be overstated. In Corey's book "Epitaph Theory" he talks about a substitute teacher who changed his life in grade ten. He had behavioural problems in school and many of the advisors and administration were thinking a "work experience or remedial type program" may be best. Other teachers didn't want to deal with him or any issues he might have so they elected just to send him to the office on a regular basis to the people who are "paid to deal with these problems." However, that was before the best teacher he ever met, Sue Veilette (who we understand has changed her name since then), told him to stay after class. This is what Corey recalls from that conversation:

---

[14] http://adamadgroup.com

"I was fully expecting her to have a talk about my behaviour and to get the regular scolding I had coming to me for being disruptive in class. Instead, she proceeded to tell me she could see signs of brilliance in me and I could easily be the smartest in the class. My behaviour was the only thing holding me back and if I just changed that I could do anything I set my mind to. WOW! That was truly a game changer for me and from that small talk I turned my life around and went from risk of failure and permanent suspension to being an honour student who went onto many personal and career successes. I had the privilege of meeting Sue over twenty years later to tell her the story and asking for permission to share it in my book. That meeting came at a time in her life when she was struggling and wondering if what she did made any difference anymore so

you can imagine how my story and encouragement changed her perspective. We shared some smiles, tears, and laughs and I had the opportunity to thank her many years after. I encourage you to thank others sooner than I did. Never underestimate the value of encouragement!"

Many times in Wai's life he was feeling down, as all of us do at times, and many of those times it was the words of encouragement from others that helped get him through those tougher times. Encouragement keeps us going, no matter the adversity that faces us. Encouragement makes people better!

We're sure all of you have an example of a time in your life when you received a word of encouragement that helped keep you going. Why does encouragement keep us going and bring out the best in

us? Encouragement gives us confidence and the ability and efficacy to believe we can do things! Psychologists say that, deep down, all people have certain desires in common. If you want to encourage people, help them fulfill these most basic, heartfelt desires.
Encouragement Gives Hope.

Most people want to:

- do the right thing. **Stand with them.**
- find better ways of doing things. **Empower them.**
- achieve things they can be proud of. **Motivate them.**
- belong to a group that achieves the extraordinary. **Invite them.**
- earn recognition for who they are and what they achieve. **Honour them.**

Encouragement turns lives around. Everybody needs somebody sometime.

One of the great things about encouragement is that you don't have to be brilliant to encourage people; you just have to have a heart for other people. Find ways to encourage others. Put your arm around them and tell them how much you appreciate them. You never know if that one good act of kindness is exactly what they need. As you encourage others, you encourage yourself.

When giving encouragement, be sure it's earned. And remember to keep it sincere, honest, appropriate, meaningful, balanced, and specific. Think of someone who has been an encouragement to you. Follow their example and pay it forward to someone you know. Don't hesitate; do it today and make a difference in someone's life.

Results

Through the years Wai has accomplished many of his dreams. From writing a song that got picked up and featured on CMT to writing multiple books and becoming a professional speaker to being a fundraiser and community advocate. Wai has also done many sports like skiing, swimming, and horseback riding and even did a week-long cattle drive one year.

He loves to combine his activities with unique fundraisers for a good cause and to promote his message to all and inspire others to rise up and support great causes around them. On August 19, 2016, Wai successfully swam two kilometres with a volunteer lifeguard by his side for 80 lengths (40 laps). She read the previous lap time posted on the white board and encouraged him to keep up the pace. She assisted him when he had to leave or re-enter the pool for a few juice breaks. For over two hours, he was able to propel himself through the water without any help. His fastest lap time was 100 meters in three minutes. Wai's team and supporters cheered him on. Several took turns ringing the lap bell. The event coordinator, Graham Specht, matched Wai's total laps between taking pictures and filming. Toward the end, some supporters hopped in and swam along for the final countdown.

Through the "Swim All The Wai" event Wai raised $1200 for the Kamloops YMCA Emergency Women's Shelter. This money was put things like their grocery budget to feed 23 people for two weeks, or three months of snacks for school kids staying at the shelter for three months. In addition to that event people can still buy Wai's book at the Kamloops YMCA at 400 Battle Street. The money will be put into their operating budget to ensure women and children have an opportunity to access a safe environment and experience the possibilities that hopefully can change their lives.

Wai has also done fundraisers for Community Living and is a speaker at many conferences on topics like "Breaking Limitations", diversity, and bullying. He loves to be a model and share his story to encourage action and involvement that can create meaningful change. Not one to shy away from a camera or promotional opportunities, Wai is often on camera or in studio for interviews for his next big event or fundraiser. All these things Wai does would be remarkable for any one person to do but to be a person with cerebral palsy and subject to discrimination and limitations that the world puts on him make Wai's accomplishments and actions even more remarkable and inspiring.

Wai has touched thousands of lives now through his work and many organizations and will continue to do so. With a renewed enthusiasm to use whatever precious time he has after his recent heart attack we expect to see even greater things in the years to come from this remarkable human being.

Our question to you is: What are you going to do to make an impact in your community and other peoples' lives?

This next section comes from a blog post Corey did March 29, 2018 titled "When Winning Just Isn't Good Enough - Dangers of Being Too Competitive"

"A GOLD MEDAL IS A WONDERFUL THING. BUT IF YOU'RE NOT ENOUGH WITHOUT IT, YOU'LL NEVER BE ENOUGH WITH IT." (from the movie "Cool Runnings" based on 1988 Jamaican bobsled team at Calgary Olympics).

The quote comes near the conclusion of the film. Derice Bannock (played by Leon Robinson) asks his coach, disgraced Olympic gold medalist Irving "Irv" Blitzer (played by John Candy) why he resorted to cheating, especially when he already had fame and fortune. Irv tries to explain that he had to keep on winning because that was his whole life. Derice can't still understand, so Irv then delivers the quote.

If you make it your sole purpose in life to just accumulate material items, wealth, and fame, you'll never be satisfied with your lot in life because you'll always want more. Sometimes, you need to just be happy and content with what you have.

If some of you are competitive like us and like to set high standards and goals for yourselves, then this message is for you. Last summer Corey spent time with Dave Klassen, National Director from Athletes in Action. Dave works as a chaplain with pro teams in Vancouver – the BC Lions, Vancouver Canucks, and Vancouver Stealth. He also oversees, trains, and directs sports chaplains across Canada in the CFL, NHL, NBA, MLS, NLL and other minor sports leagues. Moreover, he speaks at a number of events and conferences throughout the year to a variety of different audiences.

Corey originally met Dave at a breakfast meeting for which he was the keynote speaker. Given Corey's passion for high performance and his past work with sports teams, he asked to connect while Dave was in Kamloops with the BC Lions for their training camp. Immediately, Corey could tell Dave was a serious force for good. They talked at length about of sport, psychology, and performance and then, as Corey was asking questions, the conversation shifted to the "the other side of sport" or, more accurately, what life is like once an athlete's competitive career is over.

For many athletes, or people who have built an identity tied to their business or career, they move into what Dave called a "void" once they move on from that career. Corey found that fascinating and profound. The attachment to identity created a sense of worth that was only satisfied in their mind when they were performing or winning...not from just 'being.' He mentioned examples of athletes who drop into deep depression and some go as far as suicide or die shortly after leaving their careers. Some get into drug or alcohol abuse to "fill the void" and mask the pain. Most of these people figured out how to master their mind and body but never figured out how to nourish the soul - and that creates the void. Dave said his role is to give players, coaches, and others something deeper and more meaningful in their lives. He plays a big part in the motivational speeches teams use during practices and games. Dave was a competitive athlete himself and knows too well the dangers of tying your worth and identity to sport (or career) and how that can leave a void. This void is felt not just after leaving the career but can also be felt during the career. Material things and masking the pain only provide a short-term distraction but the real work must come from within. You must fill the void at a higher level - a spiritual level. We aren't talking religion here, specifically, because spirituality means a lot of things to different people and religion may be only one area that applies. Some like nature and getting into the wilderness, quiet time, meditation, or a multitude of things and that is how they connect "spiritually."

As human beings we are like an iceberg. People, external to us, see our behaviour - the end result - and, more importantly, what we choose and want them to see for the most part. Much of what they see are the physical manifestations we produce through our behaviour or goods and services we own or produce – which some equate to success. For athletes it's championships and winning; for businesspeople, it may be money and status, for example. Some may get an idea of the mental side of the person that helped get the results they see. However, the "void" that Dave talked about is normally hidden. For some, this may be mental illness against which they battle daily. Others may focus on these external measures of success which gave them the results they thought they wanted, but once reached, they realize those goal cost them their health, marriage, relationships with family and friends, and general feeling of not being happy or satisfied - the "void."

As a foundation, high self-regard is key to success in all areas of life. You can't buy it and it isn't something you win – you develop it and do certain things to build and maintain it. You can also build upon it (something the HOP® Performance Institute can help with). Gold medals are nice as are the other blessings that may come with a successful journey. But those blessings are even more meaningful when they're tied to a higher purpose and aligned with your essence further supporting and building your self-regard. Corey said this about his own personal experience:

"I know I've personally set goals and targets in my life thinking that when I get "that" or achieve "those" then I'll be happy...or at least happier. I now know that thinking is flawed. I still believe strongly in having clear goals and striving and stretching oneself to grow constantly. However, I need to check-in from time to time to ensure whatever I am doing and

striving for has a higher order purpose (another HOP) that brings meaningfulness - not just to my life but others'. It can happen in the seemingly small things the like hugs and kisses I give my daughters in the morning and at night (which, by the way, is actually a big thing). Or it may be even grander like building a school a year around the world to give children, who would not otherwise have the opportunity, to get an education and possibly use that as a springboard to a better life for them and their family."

So, CONTINUE TO EYE THE GOLD AS IT'S A WONDERFUL THING. However, IF YOU'RE NOT ENOUGH WITHOUT IT, YOU'LL NEVER BE ENOUGH WITH IT!

Corey was one posed a question on the difference between "doing things right" and "doing the right things". Below is Corey's response:

Doing the wrong things right means you're still doing something wrong. It always pays to do the right things! Doing the right things doesn't always mean things turn out as you planned but it does allow you to maintain your integrity and hold your head high in whatever the decision is. I used to always say my guiding principles in decision making were "let common sense and your conscience be your guide." I realize for some of you those of you who are employed and your organization does not seemingly operate on this principle and is more of a dictatorship, it may put you in an awkward position and possibly put your employment at risk. However, I would ask the question "what is the effect on your health of doing things you know are wrong even when done right?" Also, the long-term implications of the answer to this secondary question, not just in the short term, need to be considered. It can take years or decades to build a reputation and integrity but it only takes one bad decision to take that away or have it questioned (i.e. doing a wrong thing the right way or doing as you are told even when you know it is wrong). When in doubt take the high road. If you're worried about repercussions from an employer or boss then have a discussion and express those concerns, maybe even put those concerns in writing, and help them understand your point and be open to what they have to say before assuming you know it is wrong. I look forward to hearing other people's comments. In the meantime, keep your head held high!

Now, to do the right things means one has to be good at prioritizing. Prioritizing is a vital skill for every leader, no matter what level you are currently at or what size team, company, or organization you lead. But not every leader practices this discipline. Here are some reasons why:

It's easy to believe that if we are busy that we are achieving. But busyness doesn't equal productivity; activity does not necessarily mean accomplishment.

Setting priorities requires leaders to think ahead on a continual basis, to know what's important, to know what's coming next, and to see how everything relates to the overall vision. Plain and simple, that's a lot of hard work.

Setting priorities causes us to get out of our comfort zone at the very least and sometimes we have to do things that are painful.

The world is full of distractions and the road of many entrepreneurs is marked by taking many dead-end exits that they initially see as an opportunity but ultimately are a distraction from the path they are already on and meant to pursue and complete. This means that many entrepreneurs feel that they need to follow up on every opportunity that comes across their path. However, this takes focus away from things they are already doing and the opportunity may only be a distraction, thus taking them away from the focus of their business and, hence, dead-end exits.

For Kirk and Corey, they reflected on how easy and subtle this distraction can be. We can often get distracted by tasks or activities that are easier to accomplish but don't necessarily move us forward in business or life— like organizing an office, dealing with email, spending time on social media, following sports updates or watching TV, getting distracted with household chores or other responsibilities if you work from home, or reading another leadership or personal development book instead of getting out and meeting people.

It's not to say those things are bad in and of themselves. In fact, all of those things are quite fine but aren't the best use of our time. If we want to make an ever-increasing impact in sport, business, or life, we have to be aware of how we are utilizing our time so we can be as effective as we can possibly be—so we can be doing and giving our BEST.

As a leader, here are some important questions to ask yourself to help you evaluate your priorities[15]:

1. What is required?
We are all responsible and accountable to someone for the work we do. We also have responsibility for

---

[15] Inspired by Amy Snow - www.amysnowcoaching.com

important people in our lives like parents, a boyfriend/girlfriend, spouse, or children. The question to ask yourself is "What must I do that nobody else can or should do for me?" This list will get shorter the longer you live out this journey. If you're doing something that isn't necessary, eliminate it. If you're doing something that is necessary but not required of you personally, delegate it.

2. What gives the greatest return? As a leader, you need to be spending the bulk of your time working in your areas of greatest strength. You still need to get out of your comfort zone but stay within your strength zone. Just because you can do it, doesn't mean you should do it. That is a tough one for leaders. A suggested rule of thumb is if what you're doing can be done 80 percent as well by someone else, delegate it. Or develop

and train someone who could handle it for you. Remember that activity is not necessarily accomplishment, so don't get bogged down doing things others could be doing instead. This frees you up to lead in the ways you are best equipped. So, what can you let go of today?

3. What brings the greatest reward? This question relates to personal satisfaction. What are the things you love to do? Prioritize the things you love to do in your schedule because it will energize you and fuel you to be fully engaged and giving your best. Corey talks about this in the HOP program as what he refers to as the "Biggest Vs. Current Asset" exercise. Here we have people look at where people are currently putting their energy in and bulk of their time and compare that to where they would like to put their energy and time and what they love most in their life. Often

times we find people's current asset looks like they are spending more time and effort into things like work and time wasting activities to the detriment of things they love and prioritize like family and loved ones and hobbies and contribution activities that gives meaning and create a ripple of impact.

So here is your homework Ask yourselves these questions and write down your answers:

What is REQUIRED of me?
What gives the greatest RETURN?
What brings the greatest REWARD?

Once you've answered these questions, make a list of things that don't fit into one of the three R's. Delegate or eliminate those things.

As a leader, it's important to remember you need to help your teammates be successful. How are you helping your team live according to the Law of Priorities? How are you prioritizing and thinking ahead for your area of responsibility?

Thank you to Amy Snow for the inspiration in this section.

Priorities and Wake Up Calls

This section comes directly from James Clear, the author of the bestseller "Atomic Habits"[16], and was good enough to share directly with all of you. We are providing the links to his site for those of you interested in this line of prioritization and methods or just looking for ideas to get your head out of the weeds and be more balanced and productive.

By 1918, Charles M. Schwab was one of the richest men in the world.

Schwab was the president of the Bethlehem Steel Corporation, the largest shipbuilder and the second-largest steel producer in America at the time. The famous inventor Thomas Edison once referred to Schwab as

---

[16] The Ivy Lee Method: The Daily Routine Experts Recommend for Peak Productivity by James Clear; www.jamesclear.com

the "master hustler." He was constantly seeking an edge over the competition. [1]

One day in 1918, in his quest to increase the efficiency of his team and discover better ways to get things done, Schwab arranged a meeting with a highly respected productivity consultant named Ivy Lee.

Lee was a successful businessman in his own right and is widely remembered as a pioneer in the field of public relations. As the story goes, Schwab brought Lee into his office and said, "Show me a way to get more things done."

"Give me 15 minutes with each of your executives," Lee replied.

"How much will it cost me," Schwab asked.

"Nothing," Lee said. "Unless it works. After three months, you can

send me a check for whatever you feel it's worth to you." [2]

The Ivy Lee Method

During his 15 minutes with each executive, Lee explained his simple method for achieving peak productivity:

At the end of each workday, write down the six most important things you need to accomplish tomorrow. Do not write down more than six tasks.

Prioritize those six items in order of their true importance.

When you arrive tomorrow, concentrate only on the first task. Work until the first task is finished before moving on to the second task.

Approach the rest of your list in the same fashion. At the end of the day, move any unfinished items to a new list of six tasks for the following day.

Repeat this process every working day.

The strategy sounded simple, but Schwab and his executive team at Bethlehem Steel gave it a try. After three months, Schwab was so delighted with the progress his company had made that he called Lee into his office and wrote him a check for $25,000.

A $25,000 check written in 1918 is the equivalent of a $400,000 check in 2015. [3]

The Ivy Lee Method of prioritizing your to-do list seems stupidly simple. How could something this simple be worth so much?

What makes it so effective?

On Managing Priorities Well

Ivy Lee's productivity method utilizes many of the concepts I have written about previously. Here's what makes it so effective:

It's simple enough to actually work. The primary critique of methods like this one is that they are too basic. They don't account for all of the complexities and nuances of life. What happens if an emergency pops up? What about using the latest technology to our fullest advantage? In my experience, complexity is often a weakness because it makes it harder to get back on track. Yes, emergencies and unexpected distractions will arise. Ignore them as much as possible, deal with them when you must, and get back to your prioritized to-do list as soon as possible. Use simple rules to guide complex behavior.

It forces you to make tough decisions. I don't believe there is anything magical about Lee's number of six important tasks per day. It could just as easily be five tasks per day. However, I do think there is something magical about imposing limits upon yourself. I find that the single best thing to do when you have too many ideas (or when you're overwhelmed by everything you need to get done) is to prune your ideas and trim away everything that isn't absolutely necessary. Constraints can make you better. Lee's method is similar to Warren Buffett's 25-5 Rule, which requires you to focus on just 5 critical tasks and ignore everything else. Basically, if you commit to nothing, you'll be distracted by everything.

It removes the friction of starting. The biggest hurdle to finishing most tasks is starting them. (Getting off the couch can be tough, but once you actually start running it is much easier to finish your workout.) Lee's method forces you to decide on your first task the night before you go to work. This strategy has been incredibly useful for me: as a writer, I can waste three or four hours debating what I should write about on a given day. If I decide the night before, however, I can wake up and start writing immediately. It's simple, but it works. In the beginning, getting started is just as important as succeeding at all.

It requires you to single-task. Modern society loves multi-tasking. The myth of multi-tasking is that being busy is synonymous with being better. The exact opposite is true. Having fewer priorities leads to better work. Study world-class experts in nearly any field—athletes, artists, scientists, teachers, CEOs—and you'll discover one characteristic runs through all of them: focus. The reason is simple. You can't be great at one task if you're constantly dividing your time ten different ways. Mastery requires focus and consistency.

The bottom line? Do the most important thing first each day. It's the only productivity trick you need. [4]

FOOTNOTES

Charles M. Schwab, the president of Bethlehem Steel, is not related to the American banking and brokerage magnate, Charles R. Schwab, who is the founder of the Charles Schwab Corporation. What are the odds that two unrelated men named Charles Schwab each end up with a personal net worth over $500 million? Pretty good apparently.

It is unbelievable how hard it is to track down an original source for this story. Most stories incorrectly list the year of Lee and Schwab's meeting as 1905 or so, but 1918 seems to be the accurate year as listed in pages 118-119 of "The Unseen Power: Public

Relations: A History" by Scott M. Cutlip. Among the many books that mention reference this story are The Time Trap by R. Alec Mackenzie and Mary Kay: You Can Have It All by Mary Kay. The earliest reference I have tracked down for the story is from the 1960s. If you are aware of any earlier sources, please let me know and I will update this article accordingly.

When calculating the equivalent value of a $25,000 check from 1918 in 2015 terms, I came up with results between $390,000 and $428,000 depending on which methods and numbers are used to calculate inflation. Thus, $400,000 seems like a reasonable middle ground.

Thanks to UJ Ramdas who originally told me about the story of Charles M. Schwab and Ivy Lee. And to Cameron Herold, who shared the story with UJ.

For more tips on prioritization and habit formation please visit James Clear's we highly recommend buying his book Atomic Habits and visiting his website at www.jamesclear.com

Wai 2.0 and Legacy

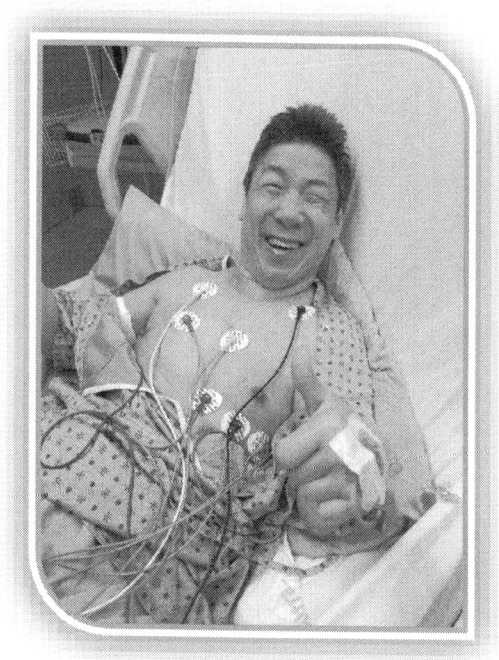

When you're 80 years old, sitting in your porch rocking chair and reflecting on life, questions such as "Did I live a useful life?" will cross your mind. There's no doubt this question will be important to you at

80, so it really should be important to you now.

Unfortunately, a lot of people make a habit of postponing life. They think that somehow, some way, somewhere at some time, life will get better. This rather poignant saying helps illustrate my point:

"First, I was dying to finish high school and start college. And then I was dying to finish college and start working. And then I was dying to marry and have children. Then I was dying for my children to grow old enough so I could return to work. Then I was dying to retire. And now I am dying and suddenly realize I forgot to live."

Isabel Moore said, *"Life is a one-way street. No matter how many detours you take, none of them leads back. And once you know and accept that, life becomes much simpler."*

"I've understood for some time that the only day I have is today. Even so, having a heart attack a few years ago crystallized that concept in my mind. Life is a one-way street. This isn't a dress rehearsal—it's a live performance.

"We need to take special care to live a useful life, starting now."

So, what does it mean to live a useful life? For Corey, the usefulness of his life is determined by:

- The relationships he forms
- The decisions he makes
- The experiences he encounters

Relationships help us define who we are and what we can become. More than almost anything else, relationships determine the kind of a life you lead. In fact, most people can trace their failures or successes back to pivotal relationships.

Our relationships with others fall into one of four categories:

1. Addition—Some relationships add to who we are.

2. Subtraction—Some relationships take a little bit out of us.

3. Multiplication—Some relationships can multiply our strengths, results and contacts.

4. Division—Some relationships can divide us.

Think about the people in your life. Where do they fit into these categories? I'm sure it wouldn't take long to put names beside each category, right? Many of the sorrows we experience spring out of relationships with the wrong people. But it is also true that some of the greatest joys we experience in life develop as the result of our relationships with the right people.

With that in mind, work to increase the time and energy you invest in the relationships that improve your life.

And, perhaps above all, work on becoming a person who improves others' lives.

Our decisions also determine the usefulness of our lives. One of my favorite quotes on making decisions comes from the great John Wooden, who said, *"Make each day your masterpiece."*

There are two ingredients necessary to make every day a masterpiece: decisions and discipline. Decision-making takes care of goal setting, but discipline also takes care of goal-getting. Decisions and discipline can't be separated; one is worthless without the other.

Since we're talking about living a useful life, let's share what Corey considers to be a few of his own life-changing decisions.

- "I am committed to continual personal growth. I believe growth is happiness, it is essential. Out of my growth I live, and out of my growth, I give."

- "I will give and serve on the front end. Many of the blessings I enjoy today are the result of the decision my wife, Margaret, and I made to try to live a life of giving with no strings attached."

- "I will exhibit a great attitude, regardless of the situation."

Virginia Satir said, *"Life is not the way it's supposed to be. It's the way it is. The way you cope with it is what makes the difference. It's not the circumstances life deals us that determine our success or failure. It's our response to it.*

"Finally, the experiences we encounter on a daily basis impact our ability to live a useful life. Joseph Campbell put it best, 'People say that what we're all seeking is meaning for life.... I think that what we're seeking is an experience of being alive.'"

Our experiences determine how fulfilling our life is, and there are four realms to every experience:

1. Entertainment—Absorbing experience through the senses

2. Educational—Participation of a person's mind or body, sometimes both

3. Escapist—Completely involves the person, like going to a theme park

4. Esthetic—Immersion in an environment but not affecting it

Jim Gilmore was spot-on when he said, *"The richest and most compelling human experiences draw from all four realms."* If you are a leader or a communicator, ask yourself: When I am communicating with or leading people, do I involve all four experiences?

Final Thoughts

If you're not doing something with your life, it doesn't matter how long it is. If you are doing something with your life, it doesn't matter how long it is. Life does not consist of years lived, but of its usefulness. If you are giving, loving, serving, helping, encouraging, and adding value to others, you have a useful life!

As true as these words are for Wai, they are equally so for great icons like Richard Branson who posted something similar on the Virgin website a while ago under the title "Don't live for the weekend, live for every single day."[17] In the article Branson says:

"One thing I've noticed after decades in business – far too many people just

---

[17] https://www.virgin.com/richard-branson/friday-your-favourite-day-work

live for the weekend. They tolerate their jobs as a means to an end and only really enjoy their life when they're not at work.

"When I was writing my new autobiography, Finding My Virginity, I had to edit it quite ruthlessly, make lots of changes and sometimes change its direction. It made me think, you also have this creative control over your life as you're going along – it's your story after all. You can't change yesterday, but now and tomorrow is still up for grabs.

"If you don't like where you are in life or what you are doing every day, then change it. It really is that simple. Everyone has responsibilities and commitments but don't be afraid to pursue your passions. If you don't enjoy your job, think about getting a new one, retraining or starting your own venture. You may not be able to walk into your perfect job right at this

moment, but you can start putting the building blocks in place to get you closer to your dream. Even by making the first step, you are one step closer than you were. If you're not sure what your dream is, then get out there and try new things and see what you enjoy.

"I didn't enjoy school and I wasn't very good at it as I struggled with my dyslexia and many teachers just thought I was lazy. This spurred me to leave as soon as I could and set up my own Student magazine, and later Virgin Records. Even back then I had big dreams of going into many different industries to help students – banking, travel, and anywhere where young people didn't have a voice. It is truly incredible looking back at how this dream morphed into what Virgin has become today. I've disrupted stagnant industries where I thought things could (and should) be done

better. It's this desire not to accept the status quo that has built the Virgin brand.

"I've always set myself short-term and long-term goals and I make sure I write them down. I tick them off as I go, which keeps me motivated. If there's something you want, you have to work hard to get it. Making a list keeps me focused on the bigger picture. I also remind myself of the things I'm grateful for and this helps keep my priorities in check.

"Don't live for the weekend, live for every single day."

Always remember to be irresistible!

Drago Adam's Monday Motivator on June 22, 2015 says this:

Some people, regardless of what they lack—money, looks, or social connections—always radiate with energy and confidence. Even the most skeptical individuals find themselves enamored with these charming personalities.

These people are the life of every party. They're the ones you turn to for help, advice, and companionship.

You just can't get enough of them, and they leave you asking yourself, "What do they have that I don't? What makes them so irresistible?"

The difference? Their sense of self-worth comes from within.

Irresistible people aren't constantly searching for validation, because they're confident enough to find it in themselves. There are certain habits they pursue every day to maintain this healthy perspective.

Since being irresistible isn't the result of dumb luck, it's time to study the habits of irresistible people so that you can use them to your benefit.

Get ready to say "hello" to a new, more irresistible you.

1. They Treat EVERYONE With Respect

Whether interacting with their biggest client or a server taking their drink order, irresistible people are unfailingly polite and respectful. They understand that—no matter how nice they are to the person they're having lunch with—it's all for naught if that person witnesses them behaving badly toward someone else. Irresistible people treat everyone with respect because they believe they're no better than anyone else.

2. They Follow The Platinum Rule

The Golden Rule—treat others as you want to be treated—has a fatal flaw: it assumes that all people want to be treated the same way. It ignores that people are motivated by vastly different things. One person loves public recognition, while another loathes being the center of attention.

The Platinum Rule—treat others as they want to be treated—corrects that flaw. Irresistible people are great at reading other people, and they adjust their behavior and style to make others feel comfortable.

3. They Ditch The Small Talk

There's no surer way to prevent an emotional connection from forming during a conversation than by sticking to small talk. When you robotically approach people with small talk this puts their brains on autopilot and prevents them from having any real affinity for you. Irresistible people create connection and find depth even in short, everyday conversations. Their genuine interest in other people makes it easy for them to ask good questions and relate what they're told to other important facets of the speaker's life.

4. They Focus On People More Than Anything Else

Irresistible people possess an authentic interest in those around them. As a result, they don't spend much time thinking about themselves. They don't obsess over how well they're liked, because they're too busy focusing on the people they're with. It's what makes their irresistibility seem so effortless.

To put this habit to work for you, try putting down the smart phone and focusing on the people you're with. Focus on what they're saying, not what your response will be, or how what they're saying will affect you. When people tell you something about themselves, follow up with open-ended questions to draw them out even more.

5. They Don't Try Too Hard

Irresistible people don't dominate the conversation with stories about how smart and successful they are. It's not that they're resisting the urge to brag. The thought doesn't even occur to them because they know how unlikeable people are who try too hard to get others to like them.

6. They Recognize The Difference Between Fact And Opinion

Irresistible people handle controversial topics and touchy subjects with grace and poise. They don't shrink from sharing their opinions, but they make it clear that they're opinions, not facts. Whether discussing global warming, politics, vaccine schedules, or GMO foods, irresistible people recognize that many people who are just as intelligent as they are see things differently.

7. They Are Authentic

Irresistible people are who they are. Nobody has to burn up energy or brainpower trying to guess their agenda or predict what they'll do next. They do this because they know that no one likes a fake.

People gravitate toward authentic individuals because they know they can trust them. It's easy to resist someone when you don't know who they really are and how they really feel.

8. They Have Integrity

People with high integrity are irresistible because they walk their talk, plain and simple. Integrity is a simple concept but a difficult thing to practice. To demonstrate integrity every day, irresistible people follow through, they avoid talking bad about other people, and they do the right thing, even when it hurts.

9. They Smile

People naturally (and unconsciously) mirror the body language of the person they're talking to. If you want people to find you irresistible, smile at them during conversations and they will unconsciously return the favor and feel good as a result.

10. They Make An Effort To Look Their Best (Just Not Too Much Of An Effort)

There's a massive difference between being presentable and being vain. Irresistible people understand that making an effort to look your best is comparable to cleaning your house before company comes—it's a sign of respect for others. But once they've made themselves presentable, they stop thinking about it.

11. They Find Reasons To Love Life

Irresistible people are positive and passionate. They're never bored, because they see life as an amazing adventure and approach it with a joy that other people want to be a part of.

It's not that irresistible people don't have problems—even big ones—but they approach problems as temporary obstacles, not inescapable fate. When things go wrong, they remind themselves that a bad day is just one day, and they keep hope that tomorrow or next week or next month will be better.

Bringing It All Together

Irresistible people did not have fairy godmothers hovering over their cribs. They've simply perfected certain appealing qualities and habits that anyone can adopt as their own.

They think about other people more than they think about themselves, and they make other people feel liked, respected, understood, and seen. Just remember: the more you focus on others, the more irresistible you'll be.

So, there you have it: Live for every day, not just the weekend; be irresistible; and if you're not doing something with your life, it doesn't matter how long it is. Life does not consist of years lived, but of its usefulness. If you are giving, loving, serving, helping, encouraging and adding value to others, you have a useful life!

We hope Wai's story and message rings true and inspires you. Corey's first book was titled "Epitaph Theory: How Do You Want To Be Remembered?" and it begs the question of what you feel your legacy will be and how do you want to be remembered? The choices you make today shape not only your destiny but the future of others. Choose wisely!

So how do you want to be remembered? What are you prepared to do starting today to create the maximum impact in this world and to move into your 'What If' potential?

Call to Action

We hope this book has inspired you to take the first steps on your own journey to break your own limitations.

Most people, when they read a book like this, will be inspired for a short term, but not live into their new possibilities. We encourage you to set some goals that stretch you and break through the obstacles and challenges you have in front of you.

In order to be successful, you need to do what the less-successful are unwilling or unable to do - take action.

As part of our mission and ongoing commitment to you, we invite you to reach out to us personally to share your story so we can support you and help hold you accountable to the new goals you are setting for yourself.

To get a hold of us, please email:
info@capleadership.com

To subscribe to our newsletter, please email:
corey@HOPPerformanceInstitute.com

For more information on the work we do, please visit:
www.breakinglimitations.ca
www.CAPLeadership.com
www.HOPPerformanceInstitute.com

Authors

Wai Hung Ma, Limit Breaker-Speaker-Coach

Wai is a man who continually lives his life by Breaking Limitations. He is an entrepreneur and professional speaker. Despite being born with the twin scourges of multiple sclerosis and cerebral palsy he has developed a positive philosophy by which he has changed from being helpless to getting more from life. It becomes a matter of risk: "…as you take more risk, you will fail from time to time, but your failures will lead to success, and you will live life fully."

Wai's infectious enthusiasm for whatever he is doing is contagious. As he says: "You have the power to choose the kind of energy that you wish to attract into your life. Positive energy is the result of positive thoughts. You have the power to choose." Wai has chosen a career in speaking when there was a time in his past when many doubted he would ever be able to even communicate clearly. Wai is surrounded by a great support structure of family and friends who are inspired by his attitude and determination to make a difference in others lives by sharing his experience.

Corey Sigvaldason, ELP, CBB, MBA, PhD Student – Thought Leader on High Performance and Founder of HOP®

Corey is known for stretching people and organizations to grow into their potential by thinking "WHAT IF…" Corey brings a great deal of experience and energy to his clients. He is a national speaking champion, author, speaker, and trainer. Corey has helped thousands of businesses over the years start, grow, or sell their business and has worked with municipalities, provinces, and nations and led local, provincial and national organizations.

Corey now shares his experience and knowledge through the HOP® Performance Institute and HOP® Performance Leadership programs worldwide. Corey has worked with a number of clients ranging from sole proprietors to Fortune 500 companies like Future Shop/Best Buy & PWC and he has worked with a variety of industries from manufacturing to education, from retail to many others. Corey also sits on a number of boards and contributes his knowledge, experience, and network with a number of organizations and mentors many people as part of his passion to change the world.

Kirk Baethke, Diploma in Broadcast (Hons.), BGS – Expert in Residence, Business Communication

Kirk has been a life-long communicator – starting out by playing with his parents' tape recorder when he was 2, moving on to winning public speaking competitions at 7, then volunteering at local radio and television stations in his teens. Subsequently, with an honours diploma in Broadcast Arts in-hand, Kirk embarked on a 26-year on-air career in radio and television. During that time, Kirk has gained experience in sales & marketing, new media, website development and management, graphic design, plus management and leadership.

Most recently, he spent 6 years as a Supervisor/Manager with one of Canada's largest telecom companies. Over that time, his teams consistently scored at the top of the company's national departmental engagement scores and he was involved in multiple initiatives to improve and evolve corporate culture.

His expertise in connecting and communicating with diverse audiences, a love of language, a keen interest in sport, plus his managerial experience, have combined to stir a passion for authentic, open leadership and effective personal and organizational communication – two of the core tenets of HOP®.

Booking Keynotes, Other Books, and Resources

All three authors are available for keynote speeches and other speaking engagements. For more information, contact our team at info@CAPLeadership.com.

You can also visit our websites for a list of topics for potential keynotes:
www.breakinglimitations.ca
www.CAPLeadership.com
www.HOPPerformanceInstitute.com

For personalized signed copies of previous books by Wai and Corey, contact our team at info@CAPLeadership.com:

Wai Hung Ma

    "Motivation"
    "Breaking Limitations"

Corey Sigvaldason

"Epitaph Theory - How Do You Want To Be Remembered?"
"No-Leap Webfoot"

Made in the USA
Middletown, DE
27 June 2019